T]

MW01278005

The War That Divided the United States

By Lance T. Stewart

Table of Contents

Introduction

"From whence shall we expect the approach of danger? Shall some trans-Atlantic military giant step the earth and crush us at a blow? Never. All the armies of Europe and Asia...could not by force take a drink from the Ohio River or make a track on the Blue Ridge in the trial of a thousand years. No, if destruction be our lot we must ourselves be its author and finisher. As a nation of free men we will live forever or die by suicide."

Abraham Lincoln

Myths About the Civil War

What do you think you know about the Civil War? If you remember what you learned in your high school history class, you probably know that the southern states fought the northern states in a number of horribly bloody battles. You might even remember the names of a few of the more famous battles, like Antietam, or Gettysburg.

You know that Abraham Lincoln freed the slaves and was assassinated by John Wilkes Booth. But what else have you learned about the Civil War since you left school?

There are a lot of popular myths and misconceptions about the Civil War that get printed in books or in Internet blog posts and lists by careless writers repeating hearsay as fact. Why does this happen? Well, for one thing, the Civil War continues to fascinate Americans. Apart from the Revolution, it is the only war ever fought on American soil, and considering that it happened just one hundred and fifty years ago, there's a good chance that you've met someone whose grandparents were alive when it happened. In fact, the last known veteran of the Civil War didn't die until 1965—so if you were born before that year, it is possible that you yourself have met someone who wore the Union blue or Confederate grey in your lifetime.

There is also the fact that the Civil War changed the nation in a number of ways, many of which still have a direct impact on the society that Americans live in today. Prior to the Civil War, a person from South Carolina would think of him or herself as a South Carolinian first, and as an American second. After the war, state loyalty became a secondary matter to national identity. Writer Shelby Foote notes that U.S. ambassadors and representatives abroad used to refer to the country as "these United States" before the war; only after the war did they begin referring to "*the* United States". Before the Civil War, the country was polarized north and south; after the south was defeated, and more and more Americans began settling the frontier, the axis shifted east and west.

Then there is the lingering impact which the Civil War had on the lives of black Americans and of whites living in the south. This is perhaps the most significant factor that affects our ability to examine the Civil War objectively, and that sometimes gives rise to popular misinformation on the subject. Slavery was technically illegalized by the war's end, but for many years in the south it continued in practice. Between the end of the Civil War and the outbreak of World War II, hundreds of thousands of blacks in the south were forced to work for rich white farmers because they had been falsely arrested under the "black codes"—laws which were purposefully designed to ensure that most blacks were breaking the law just by existing. The lives and movements of blacks in the south were, for many years after slavery ended, controlled nearly closely as when they had been slaves. Every southern state except for Arkansas and Tennessee had laws like this in place during the late nineteenth and early twentieth centuries. Not until after the Civil Rights Era of the 1960's did blacks in the south begin to see a degree of genuine legal equality with whites. But the systematic racism that is still present in the United States is a direct consequence of slavery and of the legal inequities that blacks faced for decades afterward. Examining racism makes many people uncomfortable, and that discomfort has given rise to popular myths about the Civil War, such as that the Confederate states seceded because of issues like tariffs and states rights. As we will discover in this book, however, slavery was far and away the most important political issue in the United States in the decades leading up to the war, and it was unquestionably the reason that the southern states attempted to leave the Union.

What are the other myths about the Civil War? One of them is that the North went to war with the South to end slavery. While it is perhaps understandable to conclude that if the South fought to preserve slavery, the North must have fought to abolish it, that is not precisely the case. Most people in the North were content for slavery to exist in the south, and only wanted to prevent slavery from spreading into the newly acquired American states and territories in the west—not because they considered slavery to be wrong, but because they did not want less wealthy white settlers to have to compete with the free labor that slave owners would bring with them if they were to settle in the frontier with their human property. True abolitionists were a small minority in the nineteenth century. Even Abraham Lincoln felt that the purpose of the war was to preserve the Union and prevent the southern states from forming their own country. Ending slavery was a secondary goal to ending secession.

The Civil War is a dividing line in the history of the United States. It is important to remember that when the war broke out, the nation was only a few decades old. The generation of people that fought and witnessed the Civil War were the children and grandchildren of the generation that fought the Revolutionary War. When Abraham Lincoln served his term in Congress as a Representative from Illinois, he served alongside John Quincy Adams, son of John Adams, one of America's founding fathers. Why is this important? Because the societal issues that led to the war did not arise suddenly just before Confederate soldiers fired on Ft. Sumter in April of 1861. They were the same issues that John Adams and Thomas Jefferson were debating when the U.S. Constitution was drafted—issues that most of the founding fathers recognized had the potential to tear the country apart. In the eighty years that passed between the drafting of the First Amendment and the passing of the Thirteenth Amendment, sectional conflicts between north and south grew more and more divisive, until war seemed the only possible outcome. The United States that we know today was birthed, not in 1776, but in 1865. And in order to better understand the conflicts that divide the United States today, one must gain a deeper appreciation of the fact that they are the same conflicts Americans have been wrestling with throughout the nation's history—

that, indeed, they were present from the moment the United States came into being.

We tend to find wars easier to understand when there are clearly defined villains and heroes, with one side of the conflict being obviously in the right and the other side simplistically in the wrong. In some cases, it seems easy to make this kind of distinction: for instance, we tend to think of the second World War primarily in terms of the genocidal Nazis and their allies versus the rest of the world, all of whom understood that the Nazis were evil. Aspects of the conflict that are difficult to reconcile with this narrative, such as the fact that the United States imprisoned thousands of its own citizens who were of Japanese descent in internment camps, tend to be conveniently overlooked or dismissed. Likewise, on its surface, the American Civil War appeared to be a straightforward, morally motivated conflict, because it resulted in the abolition of slavery. But the truth is much more complicated, and though heroic actions and individuals are present in the historical record, the agendas that motivated the war on both sides had little to do with moral concerns of any kind.

Let us return briefly to the most enduring myth about the Civil War: namely, the theory that the South went to war with the Union, not to defend slavery, but to defend states' rights. While this is not the case, understanding the issue of states' rights is crucial to understanding the Civil War, because it explains why the southern states felt that secession from the Union was morally and legally justifiable.

In the nineteenth century, the southern attitude toward the relationship between individual states and the federal government reflected an anti-federalist political philosophy that originated with the nation's founding, when Thomas Jefferson split with Alexander Hamilton and formed the first American political party. Southern politicians believed that, just as the American colonies had a moral and natural right to reject the authority of the British king once Parliament began interfering with colonial self-rule, any state whose right to self-rule was interfered with by the federal government had a right to leave the Union and declare itself independent and autonomous.

To put it more simply: the south wanted slavery. The economy of the south was dependent on slave labor—so dependent, in fact, that after the slaves were freed, they saw no way to transition to an economic model that did not depend on a massive, unpaid labor force, which led to the de facto enslavement of hundreds of thousands of free blacks in the decades after the war. Long before slavery was made illegal, however, southern slave owners felt threatened by the growing anti-slavery sentiment in the north. For the most part, anti-slavery factions were only fighting to prevent the spread of slavery to the western frontier, and were content to let slavery continue in the south. However, southern slave owners believed that unless slavery spread to the west, it would eventually die out in the south. Therefore, the south felt that any attempt by the federal government to limit slavery in the west indicated that the federal government did not represent the south's best interests. And where pro-slavery interests were united with anti-federalism, the result was secession. The proof of this is that not all slave states seceded and joined the Confederacy. In the border states—Maryland, Delaware, Kentucky, and Missouri—slavery was legal and popular, but secession was not.

In any event, the question of why, precisely, the South was going to war, and what it hoped to achieve by doing so, was answered by Alexander Stephens, the vice-president of the Confederacy, during a speech given in March of 1861 in Savannah, Georgia, shortly after South Carolina and several other states announced their secession, and just before Southern troops fired on Ft. Sumter. The speech came to be known as the "Cornerstone Speech", on the basis of the quote which appears below:

"The prevailing ideas entertained by him and most of the leading statesmen at the time of the formation of the old constitution, were that the enslavement of the African was in violation of the laws of nature; that it was wrong in principle, socially, morally, and politically. It was an evil they knew not well how to deal with, but the general opinion of the men of that day was that, somehow or other in the order of Providence, the institution would be evanescent and pass away. This idea, though not incorporated in the constitution, was the prevailing idea at that time. The constitution, it is true, secured every essential guarantee to the institution while it should last, and hence no argument can be justly urged against the constitutional guarantees thus secured, because of the common sentiment of the day. Those ideas, however, were fundamentally wrong. They rested upon the assumption of the equality of races. This was an error. It was a sandy foundation, and the government built upon it fell when the 'storm came and the wind blew.'

"Our new government is founded upon exactly the opposite idea; *its foundations are laid, its corner-stone rests, upon the great truth that the negro is not equal to the white man*; that slavery subordination to the superior race is his natural and normal condition. This, our new government, is the first, in the history of the world, based upon this great physical, philosophical, and moral truth." [Emphasis added.]

Not all of those who opposed slavery did so for the reasons that Stephens credited them with— the belief that slavery was a "physical, philosophical, and moral" wrong was held by only a small handful of abolitionists. Some of those who opposed slavery were merely resentful of the fact that the non-voting slave population in the South artificially inflated the representative voting power of the slave states in Congress. But as the southern economy became more dependent on slave labor, southern rhetoric around slavery became correspondingly more extreme. Not content to argue simply that the south could not do without slaves' unpaid labor, southern slavery advocates like Stephens argued that slavery was a "positive good", and that abolitionists were defying the natural order and the will of God. Ironically, southerners were more likely than most northerners to see the debate over slavery as a conflict between good and evil—with slave owners being on the side of good.

Abraham Lincoln's views on slavery were typical for most anti-slavery northerners of his era. Personally and privately, he believed that slavery was a moral evil, and that the institution should be ended, but he was not an abolitionist, and in his politics he opposed only the spread of slavery, not its existence as a whole. Abolitionists believed that slavery should be ended by any means necessary, regardless of how slave owners felt about it. Lincoln was more conservative. Like many of the anti-slavery founding fathers, he had a high regard for property rights, and considered that any attempt by the federal government to deprive slave owners of their human property without their consent or without compensation would be unconstitutional.

Before he became president, Lincoln favored systems that would abolish slavery gradually, with cash compensation for slave owners who relinquished their slaves voluntarily. After he became president, he justified his efforts to end slavery by arguing that doing so was the only way to bring the Civil War to an end. Shortly before the Emancipation Proclamation was publicly announced, Lincoln wrote to a New York newspaper, outlining his reasoning for freeing slaves in the south in such a way that put a careful distance between the legal measures he was taking and the more extreme stance of the abolitionists:

"If I could save the Union without freeing any slave, I would do it; and if I could save it by freeing all the slaves, I would do it; and if I could save it by freeing some and leaving others alone, I would also do that. What I do about slavery and the colored race, I do because I believe it helps to save the Union; and what I forbear, I forbear because I do not believe it would help to save the Union.

"I have here stated my purpose according to my view of official duty; and I intend no modification of my oft-expressed personal wish that all men every where could be free."

The Emancipation Proclamation was an executive order issued under Lincoln's special war time powers which declared the legal freedom of all slaves in the states which had seceded from the Union. The border states which had remained loyal to the Union were not affected. Slavery was not ended throughout all of the United States until the Thirteenth Amendment to the Constitution was voted into law three years later by Congress. Again, the principle goal of the North in going to war with the South was not to end slavery, but to prevent the southern states from dissolving their ties with the Union. Outlawing slavery was only a means to that end. Lincoln believed that by ending slavery in the South, the Union could re-form as a more cohesive whole—one in which the regional divisions which had conflicted the country since its creation would be done away with, and no more internal wars would be fought.

The History of the Abolitionist Movement in the United States

The abolitionist movement in the decades leading up to the Civil War created enough open opposition to slavery over the course of the nineteenth century to make the slave owners of the South feel that their way of life was under threat. It was in response to this threat that the southern states seceded from the Union and formed the Confederacy. Abolitionists were never a majority in most parts of the country— their regional stronghold was in New England— but by holding rallies, publishing newspapers, writing novels, and creating memoirs of slave life from the perspective of free blacks who had escaped from their masters, they disseminated important information about the abuses and evils inherent in slavery that helped to create popular support for the Union cause.

Slavery had existed in the American colonies since the seventeenth century. The first American slaves were transported to Jamestown, Virginia, as the property of the settlers of Britain's first New World colony; the first

American slave ship began transporting kidnapped African victims of the slave trade to America in 1636. Slavery was abolished in France and England before it was abolished in their colonies, which resulted in the slave trade flourishing in the Americas even though the abolitionist movement was gaining strength in Britain by 1783. Owing to the efforts of William Wilberforce, a British crusader for the abolitionist movement who formed the Coalition for the Abolition of the Slave Trade, slavery was illegalized throughout the British Empire in 1807. During the Revolutionary War, the British offered freedom to any American slaves who wished to defect to the Loyalist side, and a small number of slaves managed to get passage to England on British ships by the war's end, while others immigrated to Loyalist strongholds in Canada. Others, however, we re-captured by their American masters when America won the war, including at least three women who were slaves of George Washington.

American abolitionism had its roots in both religious based reform movements and in philosophical and moral theories developed during the Enlightenment era of the eighteenth century. Slavery was illegal in the state of Rhode Island between 1652 and 1700, due to Puritan religious influences, before it was re-instated by slave interests; during the same period, slavery was illegal in Georgia, before the colonial government capitulating to the same pressures.

Many of the founding fathers who designed the Declaration of Independence and the Constitution were anti-slavery in their sentiments, as Alexander Stephens acknowledged in the Cornerstone Speech, but their regard for property rights, and the need to present the delegates from the southern colonies with a document they would be willing to ratify, prevented slavery from being illegalized at the nation's birth. Between 1777 and 1804, all of the northern states had abolished slavery legally, though the Fugitive Slave clause in the

Constitution forced those states to return escaped slaves to their owners in the south. The slave trade—that is, the importing of slaves from Africa or other foreign countries—was made illegal in the Constitution, with a provision that the ban would not be enforced for twenty years, beginning in 1808.

There was a feeling in the United States in the eighteenth century that slavery was a necessary evil for the present that would eventually die out on its own. However, as technological advances like the cotton gin made the south the world's leading producer of cotton, the rhetoric around slavery changed, and pro-slavery advocates began to claim that slavery was inherent in the divine order, with whites having a Christian duty to wield dominance over the mentally inferior black race. Those who supported slavery, southerners in particular, took deep offense to the abolitionists' assertion that slavery was a sin according to the theology of the Christian religion. In the nineteenth century, abolitionism had a reputation as an extremist movement akin to anarchism; there were more than four million slaves in the United States by the beginning of the Civil War, and southern politicians claimed that abolitionists were attempting to incite the slave population to mass riots, in which their white owners would be slaughtered. Even many of those who opposed slavery believed that abolitionists did more harm than good to the anti-slavery cause, because they inflamed emotional reactions on both sides of the issue.

The most famous instance of the dissemination of abolitionist propaganda in literary form was the publication of the novel *Uncle Tom's Cabin* in serial form in newspapers, beginning in June of 1851. The novel was partially inspired by the Fugitive Slave Act of 1850. Though the original Fugitive Slave Act, written into the Constitution, required free states to return runaway slaves to their owners, some white communities defied the law, allowing escaped slaves to live in their towns peacefully. The Act of 1850 reaffirmed the

Constitutional clause and imposed harsh penalties on government officials who did not cooperate with it. This infuriated abolitionists, who feared that soon every free citizen would be legally compelled to assist in returning slaves to their owners.

Stowe's novel was also inspired by the memoirs of Josiah Henderson, who had been a slave in Maryland, but had escaped, and re-settled in Canada, where slavery was illegal under British law. Reactions to Stowe's novel, which depicted intense cruelty and abuse practiced by slave owners against their victims in melodramatic literary style, were intense and emotionally charged. The style of the book is evident in the language Stowe employs in the section quoted below:

"Well, here's a pious dog, at last, let down among us sinners! -- a saint, a gentleman, and no less, to talk to us sinners about our sins! Powerful holy critter, he must be! Here, you rascal, you make believe to be so pious, -- didn't you never hear, out of yer Bible, 'Servants, obey yer masters'? An't I yer master? Didn't I pay down twelve hundred dollars, cash, for all there is inside yer old cussed black shell? An't yer mine, now, body and soul?" he said, giving Tom a violent kick with his heavy boot; "tell me!"

In the very depth of physical suffering, bowed by brutal oppression, this question shot a gleam of joy and triumph through Tom's soul. He suddenly stretched himself up, and, looking earnestly to heaven, while the tears and blood that flowed down his face mingled, he exclaimed, "No! no! no! my soul an't yours, Mas'r! You haven't bought it, -- ye can't buy it! It's been bought and paid for, by one that is able to keep it; -- no matter, no matter, you can't harm me."

Uncle Tom's Cabin was banned in many parts of the south (along with any other form of printed material that criticized slavery). Southern slave owners, appalled by the novel's clumsy depiction of both slaves and whites, insisted that the novel was inaccurate, even slanderous. A sub-genre of reactionary literature was born as a result, as southern writers penned books such as *Aunt Phyllis's Cabin,* sentimental depictions of slave life that featured simple-minded, childlike slaves who were incapable of solving any problems without appealing to their kindly white masters for assistance. Such books claimed to represent slavery "as it really was". Nonetheless, Stowe's book was a best-seller nationwide and overseas, and it sparked intense dialogue around the slavery issue in the north. (Today, however, owing to the racial caricatures Stowe employed, the novel is studied for its historical, rather than its literary value.)

Another abolitionist writer whose work influenced feeling against slavery was Frederick Douglass, an orator and politician who had been a slave in Maryland, and had escaped to freedom when he was a teenager. His first biography,

Narrative of the Life of Frederick Douglass,
depicted the abuses he had suffered at the hands
of over-seers and owners. It also detailed his
efforts at self-education, and his escape to the
north. The book was so influential that many
pro-slavery advocates, including one of his
former masters, insisted that the writing was too
eloquent and intelligent to have been produced
by a black person. The portion of the book
reproduced below refers to some of Douglass's
first encounters with literature after he had
finished teaching himself to read:

"I was now about twelve years old, and the
thought of being a slave for life began to bear
heavily upon my heart. Just about this time, I got
hold of a book entitled "The Columbian Orator."
Every opportunity I got, I used to read this book.
Among much of other interesting matter, I found
in it a dialogue between a master and his slave.
The slave was represented as having run away
from his master three times. The dialogue
represented the conversation which took place

between them, when the slave was retaken the third time. In this dialogue, the whole argument in behalf of slavery was brought forward by the master, all of which was disposed of by the slave. The slave was made to say some very smart as well as impressive things in reply to his master-things which had the desired though unexpected effect; for the conversation resulted in the voluntary emancipation of the slave on the part of the master.

"In the same book, I met with one of Sheridan's mighty speeches on and in behalf of Catholic emancipation. These were choice documents to me. I read them over and over again with unabated interest. They gave tongue to interesting thoughts of my own soul, which had frequently flashed through my mind, and died away for want of utterance. the moral which I gained from the dialogue was the power of truth over the conscience of ever a slave holder. What I got from Sheridan was a bold denunciation of slavery, and a powerful vindication of human rights. The reading of these documents enabled me to utter my thoughts, and to meet the arguments brought forward to sustain slavery; but while they relieved me of one difficulty, they brought on another even more painful than the one of which I was relieved. The more I read, the more I was led to abhor and detest my enslavers. I could regard them in no other light than a band of successful robbers, who had left their homes, and in a strange land reduced us to slavery. I loathed them as being the meanest as well as the most wicked of men. As I read and contemplated the subject, behold! That very discontentment which Master Hugh had predicted would follow my learning to read had already come, to torment and sting my soul to unutterable anguish. "

Doubts as to Douglass's ability to have written such an eloquent book, despite his extensive learning, reflected the fact that beliefs in racial equality were not widespread in the nineteenth century, even amongst abolitionists. Many who opposed slavery believed that, while black people had the moral right to live free and pursue life, liberty, and happiness, they were nonetheless intellectually and morally underdeveloped in comparison to whites. Some doubted whether slaves were even truly human, or that they possessed a soul, and as a consequence, did not bother to give them religious instruction. This was in direct contradiction of the keen interest that many slaves took in spiritual matters. Some owners permitted slaves to hold religious gatherings on Sundays, presided over by black preachers, but after Nat Turner's slave rebellion, these gatherings were largely curtailed, because of the fear that slaves would use social gatherings as an opportunity to organize further uprisings.

Harriet Tubman and the Underground Railroad

"I had reasoned this out in my mind; there was one of two things I had a right to, liberty, or death; if I could not have one, I would have the other; for no man should take me alive; I should fight for my liberty as long as my strength lasted, and when the time came for me to go, the Lord would let them take me."

Harriet Tubman, quoted in a biography by Sarah Bradford, 1868

The most famous abolitionist of the Civil War era is undoubtedly Harriet Tubman, a former slave who escaped to freedom when she was an adult, though her exact age at the time is uncertain; she may have been around thirty. Tubman was a visionary in both the literal and metaphorical sense of the word: when she was a child, a white slave owner, attempting to re-capture one of his runaway slaves, accidentally struck her in the head with a heavy weight that was meant for the other man. She experienced severe symptoms as a result, which are now thought to be consistent with a diagnosis of frontal lobe epilepsy. She fell asleep for long periods of time and couldn't be awakened, and she began to experience hallucinations and visions, which she believed were sent by God. Because of the cruel treatment she had received from her mistress, she had tried to run away once as a child, only to be returned to her owners. When she was an adult, she married a free man of color, and she began to fear that she would be sold and her family broken up after her master's death. In 1849, she set out on another escape attempt with two of her brothers, but owing to the difficulty of escaped slaves finding passage to the north, her brothers decided it would be safest to return, and forced Tubman to come with them. Her final, successful escape attempt, which she made alone, came shortly afterwards.

The Underground Railroad provided the route for Tubman's escape. The Railroad was the code name for a series of safe houses where persons sympathetic to the abolitionist and anti-slavery cause permitted escaped slaves to hide before they were given contact details that permitted them to reach the next house further north. The terminology of railways was used to identify the various points along the escape routes: "station masters" opened their homes or barns or churches to the escapees, who stopped at "depots" along the way where they could safely rest and eat before continuing on their journeys. "Conductors", who were often Quakers, Native Americans, or free blacks, guided the fugitives from one station to the next. Those who provided financial support to the Railroad were codenamed "stockholders". Because the Fugitive Slave Act of 1850 made it difficult for escaped slaves to find permanent safe haven even in the north, the final point on the Underground Railroad was Canada, code named "the Promised Land". The Ohio River, which formed the geographical boundary between the slave and free states, was code named the "River Jordan". Travel conditions were harsh, and most of the journey had to be made on foot. Because most female slaves were more closely supervised than their male counterparts, comparatively few of them made escape attempts; Harriet Tubman was one of only a few women who were able to make use of the Underground Railroad to reach freedom.

Tubman's career as the most famous and successful conductor of the Underground Railroad began after her escape to Philadelphia, when she learned that her niece and niece's children were about to be sold at auction in Baltimore. After helping them escape to a nearby safe house, Tubman facilitated the escape of more of her family members. With each trip, Tubman became more confident in her knowledge of routes and safe houses. In 1851, Tubman attempted to help her husband escape, but he confessed himself contented with his lot in life and refused to come with her. Angered, and unwilling to waste the trip and the resources she had gathered on his behalf, Tubman invited other slaves to accompany her on the journey north. This began her career as the liberator, not just of her family, but of over seventy slaves during at least thirteen trips south.

Tubman's enormous success as a conductor on the Underground Railroad was owing to her extraordinary ingenuity, her confidence that God had appointed her to her task and would keep her safe, and her misleading personal appearance. She was middle aged and only five feet tall, and her knowledge of slave life on the plantations enabled her to easily pass as a slave in disguise right under the noses of her own former masters. She was anything but meek, however; her code name was Moses, and she carried a revolver with her, both for protection against slave catchers, and to make those who came on the journey with her understand the seriousness of the undertaking. Anyone who turned back put the entire operation at risk, and Tubman was willing to shoot them to prevent them from being captured and betraying the others. In the areas of the south where Tubman operated, the local slave owners began to notice that their slaves were disappearing mysteriously, but Tubman herself was never suspected; the slave owners believed that a white male abolitionist from the north must be responsible.

The most dramatic incident in Tubman's career was the Combahee River Raid in 1863. Due to her unique knowledge of navigating marshland terrain, she had for some time been a spy for the Union army, passing information to General James Montgomery, mapping regions of the South, and preparing slaves to stand ready for a signal to revolt. Tubman navigated three Union steamships carrying guns and soldiers along the route of the Combahee river in South Carolina. A number of plantations stood on the banks of the Combahee, and at Tubman's signal, Montgomery's men began burning these plantations to the ground. In the confusion, some 750 slaves, having been instructed by

Tubman to wait for her signal, rushed from their cabins and houses towards the refuge of the Union boats. Tubman's role in guiding the Union steamboats to their destination made her the first woman to lead an armed assault in American military history.

Conclusion

There are a number of contributing factors and complications that are often left out of the traditional narrative when discussing the Civil War. This book, while by no means an exhaustive or scholarly accounting of all the social, political, and economic factors involved, attempts to present the casual student of history with a far-reaching historical context for how the conditions that led to the war developed over the course of American history. For this reason, it begins with the American Revolution and the writing of the Constitution, and outlines the dominant political issues of the early to mid nineteenth century, before giving an overview of the war itself.

In your previous reading on the subject, you may not have learned that the southern states, particularly South Carolina, had been building up a justifying rhetoric for leaving the Union for many years before the firing on Fort Sumter. Likewise, you may not have learned that the it wasn't always taken for granted that the Union would fight the Confederacy, as some people believed that the rift between north and was so deep that it would be better to let the South form an independent government if it wished to. Other books on the Civil War provide in-depth accounts of all the military actions and battles fought between the Union and the Confederacy, but this book will only present the major battles in outline. Hopefully, it will serve as a satisfactory introduction to a topic that deserves much more in-depth study.

Chapter One: The Roots of the Civil War

The Early Republic

Most people think of the Civil War as a brief, contained conflict that began when the southern states seceded from the Union in 1861, and that ended when Confederate General Robert E. Lee surrendered to Union General Ulysses S. Grant at the Appomattox Courthouse in 1865. However, the roots of the conflict were established in 1787, after America won the Revolutionary War against England and began codifying the government of the new nation in the document that emerged as the U.S. Constitution. A certain division between north and south existed in the United States from its earliest days: the southern colonies and the northern colonies were markedly different societies, their economies founded on different strengths, and the political philosophies espoused by southern politicians, such as

Thomas Jefferson and James Madison, were almost diametrically opposed to those of their northern counterparts, such as Alexander Hamilton, Benjamin Franklin, and John Adams.

Most of America's founding fathers knew that the institution of slavery was unsustainable in the long run. The moral reprehensibility of slavery was felt by many of them, but even those who were less concerned about the damage inflicted on the millions of human beings who were victims of the slave trade saw the devastating effects that slavery could have on American society in future generations. Most of the Constitution's framers saw clearly that they had an opportunity to settle the question of slavery—that is, to end it—before it could impact future generations. The fact that they did not do so is partially owing to the dangerously fragile condition that the new American nation was in at the end of the Revolutionary War.

The Second Continental Congress

America had won its independence from Britain, but the nation did not yet have a true government of its own. The Second Continental Congress, which had raised a massive army of untrained volunteers and placed George Washington at their head, was not a unified body. Under the Articles of Confederation, each colony considered itself a more or less independent political body, banding together with its sister colonies solely for the purpose of driving the British out. As strange as it might sound, the Revolution was very nearly lost because the Continental Congress did not have the authority to levy and collect taxes from the individual colonies—it had no funds other than what the colonies could be persuaded to contribute voluntarily. It is, therefore, perhaps not terribly surprising that the money the colonies promised to contribute fell massively short of the money they actually gave.

As a result of Congress's inability to collect the needed funds from the colonies, George Washington was forced to spend more time writing to Congress and pleading for the money he needed to keep his army alive, much less in fighting condition, than he spent on the battlefield. Volunteers in the American army often had to supply their own weapons. Because they did not receive the pay they had been promised, they deserted in large numbers. Those who remained were often half naked, lacking coats, shirts, and shoes to shield them against the winter cold. Officers who had money often outfitted their men at their own expense, but even this did not prevent huge numbers of American soldiers from dying of exposure, starvation, and disease.

The Articles of Confederacy

"Each state retains its sovereignty, freedom, and independence, and every power, jurisdiction, and right, which is not by this

Confederation expressly delegated to the United States, in Congress assembled."

Article II of the Articles of Confederation, 1781

The Second Continental Congress operated under the authority of the Articles of Confederation, the forerunner to the Constitution of the United States. The Articles of Confederation established Congress's authority to conduct the war with Britain and negotiate with European countries such as France, and with the Native American nations, which at that time still constituted a considerable presence in North America. But the Articles of Confederation were an inherently weak governing document— weak by design, in a certain sense. The clue lies in the word "Confederation". By definition, a confederacy is a group of independent, semi-sovereign political entities that have entered a voluntarily compact for a specific goal. Said entities could leave the confederacy at any time. The lack of central authority was intentional. Each colony had its own government, capable of collecting taxes from its own residents; having only just severed ties with the tyrannical government of Britain, they were understandably wary of creating another powerful government that might attempt to restrict their liberty.

Confederacy was, in essence, the system of government the colonies had been accustomed to under colonial rule—each colony had its own royal governor and its own legislative body, and was essentially self ruling, though they each professed loyalty to their distant English king. The Revolution had largely been sparked by the fact that Parliament had chosen to levy new laws and taxes against the colonies without the consent of the individual colonial legislatures. There was no precedent in the New World for a central American authority, until George Washington took command of the Continental army—and that was deemed merely a military necessity. Under the Confederation government, mutual self-defense was considered one of the few exigencies under which the states would band together and submit to the direction of a single individual.

Federalism

But the miserable inefficacy of the Continental Congress and the Articles of Confederation to wage the war effectively was enough to convince most of the founders that a transition from confederacy to federation was essential. Due to the struggles he had faced over provisions, pay, and enlistment periods as commander of the Continental army, George Washington emerged from the Revolutionary War as a confirmed Federalist—he believed strongly in the absolute necessity of a strong central government, unified under a single elected leader, which would have the power to make laws that could, when necessary, supersede the laws and authority of the individual states. This was despite the fact that he was a southerner from Virginia, a plantation owner and slave owner—which, by rights, ought to have made him the natural political ally of confirmed anti-Federalists, like Thomas Jefferson and James Madison. Without a strong federal government, Washington felt certain that the new American nation would not be independent for long before it would dissolve in a civil war, and become easy prey for European powers eager for colonial possessions in the New World.

After the Revolutionary War, European observers expected George Washington to transition smoothly from the head of the American army to the head of the American government. Throughout European history, in the absence of a monarch or other central civilian authority, the person who wielded the greatest military power tended to consider it their right to rule the nation. But Washington was committed to republican principles of government, and he shocked the world by resigning as head of the army at the end of the war in 1781, leaving the formation of the new government to Congress. It was precisely for this reason that Congress unanimously elected Washington as the first American president in 1789. Not only had Washington been acting as the de facto American head of state throughout the war, giving him unique leadership experience, but it was felt that he could be trusted to lead a democracy without attempting to make himself a monarch. During Washington's first term as president, his personal popularity united Congress behind him; there were no political parties yet, only a group of state representatives working with the president and his cabinet to establish the necessary precedents of American government.

Rise of the Anti-Federalists

All of this changed during Washington's second term, however. Americans today have little sense of the incredible fear, even paranoia, that ran rampant in the early American government, sparked by the belief that operating secretly in Congress were monarchial spies who wished to convert the republic into a new dictatorship. This fear led to the creation of the two dominant political parties—parties which still exist today, albeit in a different form and under different names. Washington's party, the party of those who worked to build strong central government, became known as the Federalist party. Their chief members—Alexander Hamilton, from New York, and John Adams, from Massachusetts— were northerners, who supported, among other things, the elimination of slavery and the creation of a national bank, with the power to assume the debts of the states and collect taxes from the nation as a whole to pay the debt down.

The party that formed to oppose the Federalists was the party of Thomas Jefferson and James Madison—the Democratic-Republicans. While they continued to be personally loyal to George Washington, they were dismayed by his close relationship with Alexander Hamilton, who had created the national bank and the financial system that rested on the bank's power.

The office of the President, as it was laid out in the new Constitution, had been designed with Washington in mind—it reserved considerable power to the "Executive", or the President, a reflection of how trustworthy Washington was considered to be. But Jefferson and Madison began to be afraid of what would happen when Washington died. At the time, it was assumed that Washington would remain in office until his death—the Constitution made no provision for presidential term limits at the time. (The fact that presidents after Washington also limited themselves to two terms was merely out of respect for the precedent that Washington had set—the 22nd Amendment, which made the two-term limit law, was not passed until 1947, after Franklin D. Roosevelt served three terms.)

Jefferson and Madison were convinced that the reason that the Federalists in general, and Alexander Hamilton in particular, wanted to consolidate the power of the federal government (at the cost, as they saw it, of the independence of state governments) was because the Federalists were preparing to convert the government to a monarchy after Washington died or resigned his office. Jefferson believed that Hamilton had deceived Washington as to his true intentions, and that Washington had effectively become little more than a puppet for Hamilton's intentions. Washington found this deeply offensive, and it forced him to end his friendship with Jefferson. While Hamilton was no monarchist, it was true that, when Hamilton was creating the new American financial system, he expressed great admiration for monarchial European institutions, such as the Bank of England, and took their governing principles as his model. This reliance upon English systems, and his preference for the merchant economy of the northern states, gave him a reputation as a believer in monarchial and aristocratic systems. After Washington left office, Hamilton split with other members of the Federalist party, including the second American president, John Adams. Hamilton's public attacks against Adams, and his own increasing unpopularity, led to the Federalists falling from power in the election of 1800, when Thomas Jefferson took office as the third president of the United States.

Jeffersonian Democracy

What became known as "Jeffersonian democracy" dominated American politics for the next several decades. The tenor of Jefferson's politics reflected his personal situation as a longstanding member of the Virginia House of Burgesses under colonial rule, and his status as a plantation owner and slaveholder. The economy of the south was agrarian in nature. While the north had emerged as a strong merchant economy, home of the nation's first banks, and of Wall Street, the south had fewer large cities and no large banks. Its wealthiest citizens were plantation owners, who grew crops such as tobacco, wheat, corn, and cotton.

Southern politicians had especially resisted Hamilton's plans to assume state's debts and establish a central American bank because the southern states had little debt; their agrarian economy was supported on the backs of the free labor extorted from slaves. Yet, to Jefferson's mind, the ideal American citizen was not the plantation master and slave owner, but rather the "yeoman farmer"—someone who made a modest living through hard work and industry on his own little patch of farmland, far away from the corrupting influence of the big cities where crime and financial wheeling and dealing were taking place. Jefferson doubled the size of the American nation by making the Louisiana Purchase in 1803, buying all of France's territory south of Canada, extending to more than 800,000 square miles west of the Mississippi River. Jefferson saw the America of the future as a huge expanse of idyllic farmland, populated by agrarian settlers. An over-powerful central government, influenced by the agendas of politicians from the mercantile north, would necessarily be out of touch with needs and interests of such isolated farmers and small villages.

Slavery and the Constitution

In the eighteenth century, the fragility of the new American nation made it absolutely essential that all thirteen colonies unite to ratify the Constitution. Early versions of the Declaration of Independence condemned slavery as a moral outrage, but these sections were deleted from the final document. However vehemently opposed to slavery some of the framers of the Constitution may have been, they considered it more important, at that time, to present the Congressional delegates from the southern states with a document they would be willing to ratify— in other words, with a version of the Constitution which could be interpreted as upholding their right to continue to own slaves.

It is also important to mention that even the most outspoken anti-slavery men involved in America's founding, such as Alexander Hamilton, believed strongly in upholding the principle of property rights—in other words, they believed it would be tyrannical for the federal government to deprive citizens of property which they had acquired by legal means, even if that property was human. (This was not a concern unique to the eighteenth century—Abraham Lincoln had a similar regard for property rights, and his early legislative attempts to oppose slavery proposed to ease the economic loss of slaveholders by compensating them for freeing their slaves.) Because of this, the portions of the Constitution which had bearing on slavery were written in a peculiar spirit of compromise: it acknowledged the south's economic dependence on slave labor, while seeking to reserve the government's power to limit the slave trade, as well as the voting influence of the slave states.

The Constitution contains three clauses which have bearing on the institution of slavery— although it is worth noting that the words "slave" and "slavery" are not found anywhere in the Constitution. It has been argued by historians that these words were omitted on purpose, to allow future generations the opportunity to abolish slavery without having to alter the Constitution. The first and most famous of these clauses is Article I, Section 2, Clause 3— otherwise known as the "three fifths compromise". It is reproduced below:

"Representatives and direct Taxes shall be apportioned among the several States which may be included within this Union, according to their respective Numbers, which shall be determined by adding to the whole Number of free Persons, including those bound to Service for a Term of

Years, and excluding Indians not taxed, three fifths of all other Persons."

This clause establishes that, for census purposes, when determining the total population of a states, slaves were counted at 3/5ths of a free person (white or black). Because it is shocking to modern students of history to think of a black person as "counting" as only a fraction of a white person, there exists an impression that the 3/5ths compromise was supportive of slavery, but this is not the case.

The number of persons in a state counted by the census determines the number of representatives that state is entitled to elect to Congress. Anti-slavery northern Congressional delegates wanted to leave slaves out of the census altogether; this would have considerably reduced the number of slave state representatives in Congress, compared to the more population dense states in the northeast. Southern delegates wanted slaves to count the same as free men, despite the fact that slaves could not vote, because it would greatly increase the number of representatives they were entitled to.

The southern states were initially opposed to the 3/5ths compromise, but they were conciliated into supporting it when Constitutional framer Governeur Morris suggested that the amount of taxation each state was required to pay to the federal government likewise be dependent on the census numbers. Southern states accepted the decrease in their Congressional voting power in exchange for being liable for less taxation.

Article II, Section 9, Clause 1 of the Constitution provoked a nearly fatal rift in the Constitutional Congress, as it proposed that the federal government would have the power to tax and outlaw the slave trade. It reads as follows:

"The Migration or Importation of such Persons as any of the States now existing shall think proper to admit, shall not be prohibited by the Congress prior to the Year one thousand eight hundred and eight, but a Tax or duty may be imposed on such Importation, not exceeding ten dollars for each Person."

The slave trade was distinct from the institution of slavery itself—it referred to importing slaves from outside the country, be they enslaved persons previously living in Europe, or newly kidnapped Africans. The delegates from South Carolina and Georgia, the two most powerful southern states, threatened not to ratify the Constitution unless the clause was changed. An emergency committee, compromised of one delegate from each state, was assembled to break the stalemate; their proposal was that federal power to tax or limit the slave trade in any way be put on hold for twenty years, until 1808. This proved an acceptable compromise to the southern delegates.

The most notorious of the Constitutional provisions regarding slavery, and arguably the one that did the most damage in terms of human misery, was Article IV, Section 2, Clause 3, the Fugitive Slave clause, reproduced below:

"No Person held to Service or Labour in one State, under the Laws thereof, escaping into another, shall, in Consequence of any Law or Regulation therein, be discharged from such Service or Labour, but shall be delivered up on Claim of the Party to whom such Service or Labour may be due."

Under pressure to reinforce the right of individual states to make their own laws, this clause determined that slaves who escaped from slave states to free states must be returned to their owners, in recognition of the owners' property rights. This was possible because slavery was still legal in most of the northern states at the time, although measures were taken to abolish slavery in those states gradually by the early 1800's. If, however, a slave escaped to one of the American territories where slavery was not legal, that slave became free.

By the mid nineteenth century, the most important issue related to slavery would be the question of whether slavery should be legal in new states as they joined the union. In the eighteenth century, the prevalent feeling, even amongst southerners, was that slavery was abhorrent but necessary, and that it would be a good thing if economies that were dependent upon it could be weaned off it over time. This sentiment, however, would change drastically in the south during the next sixty years, as its economy became more dependent on slavery, not less, and as its identity became founded on the narrative that whites were rightfully dominant over blacks, who were, by nature, stupid, simple, and morally corrupt without white mastery. Slavery was already a rift that divided the nation. It was, in essence, a leak which the founding fathers had managed to patch for the time being—but instead of solving the problem, they had merely handed it down to future generations. The expediency of their time became the impetus for the most devastating war fought by Americans until the Vietnam War in the twentieth century.

Cotton and the Expansion of Slavery

Jefferson's vision of an agrarian nation peopled by independent farmers was not to come to pass. In 1793, Eli Whitney invented a device known as the cotton gin, a machine which quickly and efficiently separated the lint fibers of the cotton bud from its seeds, a process which formerly had to be completed by hand. As a result, the American south became the world's leading producer of cotton, which it could produce in vast quantities and sell more cheaply than anywhere else in the world, because it was grown, harvested, and processed by the free labor of slaves. The economy of the south, therefore, became more than dependent on agrarianism—it was absolutely dependent on the cotton trade, and, therefore, on slave labor. Slavery accordingly gained a new kind of cultural significance in the south. The more important slaves were to the economy, the more psychologically important it seemed to become to white slave owners to believe that slavery was not only necessary and justifiable, but morally and naturally correct, a settled hierarchy of racial supremacy instituted by God.

Increased southern economic dependence on slavery meant that southerners had a vested interest, not only in preserving the institution of slavery in the south, but in expanding slavery to the new territories and states that became part of the Union as the nineteenth century wore on. If all new territories and states were designated as free states, the legitimacy of slavery would begin to wane, endangering its survival in the south. Southerners with an economic interest in slavery would not be able to bring their slaves with them if they chose to move away from the traditional slave states. By the same token, anti-slavery politicians from the north had a vested interest in limiting the expansion of slavery to the new territories and states as much as possible; if slave owners from the south settled in the west, bringing their slaves with them, non slave owning settlers would not be able to compete with the free labor the slave owners were importing. The battle over which of the new states and territories would be free and which would allow slavery polarized the nation in the decades leading to the Civil War. And since the United States was rapidly acquiring new land from countries such as France and Mexico, the question of where slavery should be legal was constantly before the public.

The Missouri Compromise

"Be it enacted by the Senate and House of Representatives of the United States of America, in Congress assembled, That the inhabitants of that portion of the Missouri territory included within the boundaries herein after designated, be, and they are hereby, authorized to form for themselves a constitution and state government, and to assume such name as they shall deem proper; and the said state, when formed, shall be admitted into the Union, upon an equal footing with the original states, in all respects whatsoever."

Section I of the Missouri Compromise (1820)

In an attempt to settle the question of whether slavery would be legal in new lands acquired by the Union, United States senator Henry Clay of Kentucky proposed what became known as the Missouri Compromise in 1820. Both Missouri and Maine were poised to become states, and Missouri specifically wished to enter the Union as a slave state.

The so called three-fifths compromise, which had been designed as an effort to limit the voting power of the slave states, had ceased to fulfil this function within just a few decades of the Constitution being written. More than half of the white male voters in the United States lived in the north in 1820, but the rise of the cotton industry in the south, and the subsequent explosion in the demand for slave labor, meant that even with each slave counting as only three-fifths of a white person, the slave population was so vast that the southern states had become entitled to many more Congressional representatives than the northern states, despite being inhabited by fewer voters. If Missouri were to enter the union as a slave state, the slave states would possess an absolute voting majority over the free states.

In an effort to balance the influence of the slave and free states more or less equally, Henry Clay proposed that Missouri be admitted as a slave state, but that Maine be admitted at the same time as a free state. Furthermore, all the new territory that had become part of the United States as a result of the Louisiana Purchase would be divided along the 36°30′, latitudinal line; any states that formed in the area south of the line would be admitted as slave states, and any that were created in the area north of the line would be admitted as free states. (The line ran through the middle of Missouri, but Missouri was exempt from the statute and slavery was legal through the entire state.)

The Tariff of 1828 and the Nullification Crisis

By 1828, Britain was the largest importer of cotton from the south, and the wealth of the south was dependent on doing business with them. By trading cotton with Britain, importers

in the south were able to obtain British goods
more cheaply than by purchasing them from
rival manufacturers in the American north.

Four years after the War of 1812, Congress
passed the first of a series of protective tariffs—
taxes on foreign imported goods that served the
purpose of reducing competition for goods
manufactured in the United States. Because the
tariff hurt British businesses, they were unable to
buy southern cotton in the same quantities as
before, thereby impacting the southern economy
in a negative manner. The battle between
protectionists (who were in favor of the tariffs)
and those who supported free trade with Europe
dominated American politics through the 1810's
and 1820's. Free trade southerners claimed that
the tariffs were unconstitutional, on the basis of
the fact that the tariffs did not extend economic
protection to the nation as a whole, but only to
part of it; they opposed the Tariff of 1828 so
strongly that they labeled it the "Tariff of

Abominations". The deepening national division over the tariff issue resulted in President John Quincy Adams, son of American founder John Adams, losing the election of 1828 to Andrew Jackson.

Southerners were under the impression that Jackson would take measures to either end or at least reduce the protective tariffs, but because the tariffs strengthened the American economy in general, Jackson did not take immediate action against them. In 1832, he signed new legislation which reduced the tariffs somewhat, but not to the degree southerners had hoped for. South Carolina, the southern state whose economy had been most adversely affected by the tariff measures, saw more than 50,000 of its voters leave the state due to economic hardship. As a result, South Carolina held caucuses during which the question of secession from the Union was raised for the first time. Politicians such as John C. Calhoun, a South Carolinian who initially served as Andrew Jackson's vice president, espoused the belief that individual states had the right to enact nullification measures if the federal government passed laws that abrogated state's rights.

In legal terms, to "nullify" something means, essentially, to ignore it. In this case, nullification meant that the government of South Carolina announced that it would not abide by federal tariff laws; the state legislature adopted an Ordinance of Nullification, which stated that after the first of February of 1833, no state official was to enforce the tariff. South Carolina even went so far as to prepare military measures in case the federal government tried to force compliance with the tariff acts by force of arms, a possibility that was raised when Congress passed the Force Bill a month later, authorizing the government to do just that. The next day, however, John C. Calhoun and Henry Clay proposed a compromise tariff which lowered the amount of the tariff by a degree acceptable to the government of South Carolina, which averted the quasi secession crisis of the nullification measures. But Jackson recognized that the crisis had arisen as a result of a deep, nearly unbreachable rift between the south and the rest of the country, and he predicted that South Carolina would eventually attempt to leave the Union for good—probably over the issue of slavery.

Nat Turner's Rebellion

"And my father and mother strengthened me in this my first impression, saying in my presence, I was intended for some great purpose, which they had always thought from certain marks on my head and breast... My master, who belonged to the church, and other religious persons who visited the house, and whom I often saw at prayers, noticing the singularity of my manners, I suppose, and my uncommon intelligence for a child, remarked I had too much sense to be raised (and if I was, I would never be of any service to any one) as a slave.

"To a mind like mine, restless, inquisitive and observant of every thing that was passing, it is easy to suppose that religion was the subject to which it would be directed, and although this subject principally occupied my thoughts...the manner in which I learned to read and write, not only had great influence on my own mind, as I acquired it with the most perfect ease, so much so, that I have no recollection whatever of learning the alphabet—but to the astonishment of the family, one day, when a book was shewn me to keep me from crying, I began spelling the names of different objects—this was a source of wonder to all in the neighborhood, particularly the blacks."

Excerpt, *Confessions of Nat Turner*, 1831

All political and national debate regarding the issue of slavery was influenced by the fact that whites in the nineteenth century, especially in the south, feared slave uprisings and rebellions to a degree that bordered on paranoia. This paranoia was created in part by the slave-led Haitian Revolution, which ended in 1804, after thirteen years of conflict, with the founding of a free republic, governed by former slaves and free people of color. White French slave holders and plantation owners were massacred when white rule was overturned. The fear that the increasingly vast slave population of the United States would launch a similar revolt, leading to white bloodshed, led to measures such as South Carolina banning any abolitionist or anti-slavery literature, and later, prohibitions against teaching slaves to read and write. It also led to slave owners restricting slaves from gathering in groups to socialize, for fear they would use the opportunity to organize themselves for an uprising.

In 1831, just such an uprising occurred, although not nearly on the scale feared after the Haitian Revolution. Nat Turner was a highly intelligent, literate slave from Southampton, Virginia, who, since childhood, had had visions that he believed came from God. He was also a preacher who held religious meetings for slaves with his master's permission, and he voluntarily returned to one owner after making a successful escape because he believed he had received a message from God instructing him to do so.

In 1831, Turner became convinced that God had appointed him to "slay [his] enemies with their own weapons". With the assistance of four fellow slaves, he recruited seventy men, both slaves and free blacks, to form an armed unit. Hoping to inspire a slave revolt that would spread across the south, Turner and his men went from house to house, killing over sixty people, including women and children. Instead of using guns, they used weapons that would make no noise, such as knives, hatchets, and axes. Whites in the area responded swiftly, with overwhelming force and brutality. A militia was raised, which quickly defeated Turner's brigade, although Turner himself escaped and remained a fugitive for two months. Hysteria swept throughout the south, as rumors spread of "slave armies" on the march to massacre whites in cities such as Wilmington, North Carolina. Over two hundred blacks were charged and tried in court on charges of conspiracy, and hundreds more were savagely murdered by lynch mobs.

As a result of Turner's rebellion, calls were made in the General Assembly to end slavery in Virginia through a gradual system, in which the children of slave mothers were born free, but these measures were defeated. More laws were passed that explicitly banned the teaching of slaves, or even free blacks, to read and write, and it became illegal for slaves to hold religious meetings unless the minister that presided over them was white. Turner's rebellion became the justification for violent actions against abolitionists as well. Fearing that abolitionist doctrine would incite slaves to another murderous rebellion, lynch mobs attacked many abolitionists who wrote anti-slavery tracts and printed newspapers and destroyed their printing presses. The state of Georgia even went so far as to institute the death penalty for publishing any material that was guilty of inciting slaves to revolt—that is, nearly any abolitionist writing.

The Amistad

In 1839, fifty three Mende Africans from Sierra Leone were kidnapped and transported to Cuba to be sold as slaves, in spite of the fact that the international African slave trade had been largely illegalized, even in the United States. In Cuba, they were transferred to an American-built, Spanish owned schooner called *La Amistad*, which was to transport them as slaves to the Caribbean to work on sugar plantations.

However, the Mende managed to break their manacles, arm themselves with the very machetes that were intended for use in cutting sugar cane, and mount an insurrection against the crew of the ship. They killed everyone except the navigator, whom they instructed to take them back to Africa. The navigator made a show of agreeing, but instead took them to New York, where an American revenue ship took them into custody.

The legal situation surrounding the actions of the Mende was complicated by the question of their status. There were draconian penalties for slave revolts, and equally harsh repercussions for mutiny at sea—both carried the sentence of death, if the Mende were convicted. There were also jurisdictional issues at play: the Mende were being claimed as slave property by the U.S. government, the Spanish crown, the naval officers who seized the *Amistad,* and the Caribbean plantation owners who had purchased them. However, New York abolitionists came to the support of the Mende, and former president John Quincy Adams represented them before the Supreme Court, successfully making the case that, because the Mende had been kidnapped in violation of all international treaties, they were legally free men and not slaves at the time of the insurrection—which meant that they had a legal right to defend their freedom by attacking their captors. The thirty five Mende still living were allowed to return to Africa in 1842, their passage paid for a black abolitionist society in New York. The court's decision was one of the first landmark victories for the rights of blacks against the slave industry prior to the Civil War.

The Annexation of Texas

Texas was originally one of the New World colonial possessions of the Spanish empire, part of the viceroyalty of Mexico for over three hundred years. In 1821, however, Mexico fought and won a war of independence against Spain and became an independent republic. Mexico's northernmost province, Texas, which had been settled by large numbers of Anglo-Americans immigrants from the southern United States, declared its own independence from Mexico after fifteen years of unstable relations with the central Mexican government under President Santa Anna, who attempted to quell unrest in the region by banning any further settlement by Americans, and by illegalizing slavery.

In 1836, a Texan army under the command of General Sam Houston fought a victorious battle against the Mexicans at San Jacinto, and afterwards, Texas achieved independent republic status by treaty. The rest of the Mexican government, however, refused to acknowledge the treaty made between Texas and Santa Anna, and did not recognize the legitimacy of the Republic of Texas. As a result, Texas began negotiations with the United States to be annexed into the Union as a new state, which would gain them American military protection against further attempts by Mexico to reclaim the Texas territory.

The prospect of annexing Texas unto the United States was met with deep reservations by many, because the abolition of slavery by the Mexican government had not been successful, and Texas intended to enter the Union as one or several slave states. This would upset the balance between slave and free states established by the Missouri Compromise. However, territorial expansion was integral to American ideals in the early nineteenth century: obtaining more land on the western frontier for Americans to settle in had been a dream of every president since George Washington. (The view that the United States should and would eventually expand its borders to the Pacific Ocean was known as Manifest Destiny.) There was, furthermore, a deep suspicion amongst pro-slavery factions that if the United States did not annex Texas, then Britain, which was involved in mediating peace talks with Mexico, might attempt to fund Texan independence on the condition that slavery was abolished.

Northerners who opposed the annexation of Texas on the grounds that it would be a slave state were mollified by the "safety-valve" argument for the theory of diffusion. Very few of those which opposed the power of the slave states did so out of a belief in racial equality, and many people who condemned slavery as an evil were nonetheless afraid of what would happened if slavery were abolished and free blacks came to settle in the north. To such people, it seemed that Texas would provide an outlet that slaves, and later, free blacks, could be funneled into. Some abolitionists cherished the hopes that so many slaves would be transported into Texas to meet growing labor demands that the political power supporting slavery as an institution would begin to wane in the former colonial south.

In March of 1845, the president of the Republic of Texas agreed to the terms of the treaty that would annex Texas into the United States. Mexico, which still did not recognize Texas' sovereignty, had threatened to declare war against the United States if Texas was annexed. President James K. Polk offered to purchase the contested lands from Mexico to avert war, but the offer was rejected. The Mexican-American War began when Polk stationed American soldiers in territory still claimed by Mexico, instigating Mexican soldiers to attack. Polk's role in provoking the war with Mexico was challenged in Congress by Abraham Lincoln, during his single term as a member of the House of Representatives for Illinois.

The Wilmot Proviso

"Provided that, as an express and fundamental condition to the acquisition of any territory from the Republic of Mexico by the United States, by virtue of any treaty which may be negotiated between them, and to the use by the Executive of the moneys herein appropriated, neither slavery nor involuntary servitude shall ever exist in any part of said territory, except for crime, whereof the party shall first be duly convicted."

David Wilmot, presented to the House of Representatives, August 8, 1846

In 1846, in response to the acquisition of Texas and the debate over which new states and territories should be slave and which should be free, Congressman David Wilmot proposed that slavery should be illegal in all the new lands acquired from Mexico after the war—not merely Texas, but New Mexico and lower California. Wilmot's proposal took the form of a rider that was attached to a bill that Polk presented to Congress asking for three million dollars to purchase the lands from Mexico. Wilmot was among those politicians whose opposition to slavery was based on the fear that slave labor would make it difficult for non slave-owning whites to compete with slave owners economically.

The bill passed the House of Representatives with the necessary majority, but failed to pass in the Senate because Democrats in the north united with the southerners to vote against it. An alternative to the total banning of slavery in the new territories was proposed by Democrats, including Stephen A. Douglas of Illinois, who suggested that the 36°30' latitude line created by the Missouri Compromise which divided slave states from free states be extended all the way to the Pacific coast, but this restriction was also defeated in the Senate.

Ultimately, the bill requesting the three million dollars was passed, but without the proviso attached. The fact that the voting on the bill fell out, not along party lines between Whigs and Democrats, but along geographical lines dividing north from south, proved to be an ominous indicator of the growing disunity in the nation. Partisan divisiveness had characterized American politics since the election of 1800, but politicians had begun abandoning even party loyalty to vote along regional lines, a reflection of the degree to which southerners felt that the interests of their own region must take precedence over national interests.

The Compromise of 1850

South Carolina's decision to secede from the Union was not a hastily made or spur of the moment decision. The first formal action on the secession issue was taken in 1850, at the Nashville Convention, a meeting held over several days in a church in Tennessee between representatives of nine slave states: South Carolina, Virginia, Alabama, Georgia, Texas, Florida, Arkansas, Mississippi, and Tennessee. The passing of the second Fugitive Slave Act earlier that year had sparked intense, passionate speeches in Congress from those who opposed slavery. There was considerable fear amongst abolitionists that the Fugitive Slave Act would be expanded so as to require all Americans, not merely elected officials, to assist in the capture and return of escaped slaves. Speaking against the Act, Senator William H. Seward of New York made a famous anti-slavery speech in which he asserted that when it came to slavery, Constitutional law was subordinate to the "higher law" (i.e. God's law). This rhetoric outraged the Congressmen from the slave states. Sensing that the tide of national opinion was turning determinedly against slavery, they held the Nashville Convention in order to formulate a response in the event that the Wilmot Proviso was adopted and slavery was illegalized in all the western territories. The delegates to the convention were bipartisan, both Whig and Democrat southerners being present, and as a result, the moderate anti-secessionist influence prevailed. However, a group of extreme secessionists met for a second, more sparsely populated session of the convention; the attendees at the second session included future president of the Confederacy Jefferson Davis.

No action toward secession was taken that year, largely because of the so-called Compromise of 1850, a piece of legislation originally authored by Kentucky senator Henry Clay. His bill contained a series of proposals that were calculated to somewhat satisfy both pro and anti slavery interests. (The omnibus bill containing all of Clay's proposals was defeated by Congress, but each proposal was passed when submitted as separate bills.) The Compromise measures allowed Texas to enter the union as a slave state, while admitting California as a free state, and leaving the issue of slavery undecided in the New Mexico territory. The slave trade was banned in the District of Columbia, and the ban on slavery above the Missouri Compromise line was enforced, even though the line ran through the northernmost part of Texas. Every southerner in Congress opposed the ban on the slave trade in the District of Columbia, even though it did not constitute a ban on slavery itself, but they were otherwise satisfied. Their principle fear had been the ban on slavery in all of the southwestern territories, the position favored by President Zachary Taylor. Taylor, however, had recently died, and was succeeded by Millard Fillmore, who, though a New Yorker and a Whig, tended to support southern interests. Taylor's death made the Compromise of 1850 possible, and arguably postponed the outbreak of the Civil War by more than a decade.

The Kansas-Nebraska Act of 1854

"[This land shall be] created into a temporary government by the name of the Territory Nebraska; and when admitted as a State or States, the said Territory or any portion of the same, shall be received into the *Union with without slavery, as their constitution may prescribe at the time of the admission...*"

from Section 1 of the Kansas-Nebraska Act (emphasis added)

By 1854, no transcontinental railroad yet existed in the United States, though plans for one had been submitted to Congress off and on since the 1840's. The principle difficulty in organizing Congressional support to fund such a railroad lay in the question of whether the railroad would be located in the north or the south. The newly organized Nebraska and Kansas territories made the need for a railroad more pressing, as the country expanded westward into increasingly sparsely populated frontier territories. During this era of the nation's history, when the western frontier was comprised of highly isolated settler communities, railroads were crucial to banding the scattered towns and villages together, and to providing access to schools, hospitals, and markets for selling crops and livestock. Public works projects such as railroads were therefore the pet political agendas of virtually every Congressman from the west, including Abraham Lincoln.

The land that would be organized into the Nebraska and Kansas territories lay to the north of the Missouri Compromise line, and therefore, under the terms of the Compromise, it would have to be admitted to the union as non-slave territory. However, there was a growing opposition amongst pro-slavery Congressmen to allowing Kansas and Nebraska to be admitted as free territories, and some declared their resolution to prevent Nebraska and Kansas from entering the union at all unless they did as slave territories.

Stephen A. Douglas, a nationally famous orator and senator from Illinois, who would later run as the Democratic candidate against Republican Abraham Lincoln in the presidential election of 1860, was deeply invested in the railroad building issue in Nebraska. In an effort to mollify the southern Democrats into voting for the organization of the Kansas and Nebraska territories, he put forward the Kansas-Nebraska Act, which proposed that popular sovereignty should determine whether the territories were slave or free. Popular sovereignty meant, essentially, that the residents of Kansas and Nebraska would decide by vote whether or not they wanted slavery. This measure was popular with southerners, but they persuaded Douglas to include in the bill a repeal of the Missouri Compromise—which, President Franklin Pierce argued, had effectively been repealed by the Compromise of 1850 in any case.

Bleeding Kansas and the Caning of Charles Sumner

The reaction to the Kansas-Nebraska Act was intense, and in many ways violent. In the early nineteenth century, the two dominant political parties were the Whigs, who were anti slavery, favored strong central government, and were principally represented in the north and on the western frontier, and the Democrats, who were largely pro slavery, favored popular sovereignty and the rights of states to defy the rule of the federal government, and were predominantly represented by southerners.

The Nashville Convention, however, had exposed a deep rift in both parties. While southern Whigs had been a moderating influence at the Nashville Convention, effectively preventing the radical secessionists from formulating a plan for immediate withdrawal from the Union, the fact that they had participated in the convention at all demonstrated that their principle loyalty was to the south, not to their party. At the same time, a number of northern and frontier Democrats— including Stephen A. Douglas of Illinois, the author of the Kansas-Nebraska Act and the chief proponent of the doctrine of popular sovereignty—were supportive of the southern agenda to expand slavery.

Slavery was, from this point, until the outbreak of the Civil War, the single issue that dominated American politics above all others, and it necessitated a re-organization of the two parties. Southern Democrats split from the Democratic party. The Whig party dissolved entirely, and those of its members who were avowedly anti slavery re-organized as the Republican party. (In later years, the Southern Democratic party dissolved, and the Democrat and Republican parties would essentially swap names; starting in the mid twentieth century, the Democratic party became the party of the federalists, and the Republicans became the party of the anti federalists.)

Meanwhile, the issue of whether Kansas would be admitted to the union as a slave or free state was to be decided by popular sovereignty—in other words, by the votes of those settlers who lived in Kansas. However, at the time, there were no minimum residency requirements for voters—in effect, any white man of voting age who turned up at the ballot office was allowed to register his vote, even if he had only taken up residence in that state that very day. Because of this, large numbers of supporters of slavery who lived just over the state border in Missouri made the short journey to Kansas for the express purpose of swaying the vote to permit slavery. Likewise, some anti slavery proponents made the journey to Kansas from further east to sway the vote against slavery. For a time, there were two governments in Kansas—the Territorial government, composed of slavery supporters, and the Free State government, which opposed slavery. Both governments were supported by their own armed militias.

The existence of the two de facto rival governments with their miniature armies led, unsurprisingly, to considerable tension, which culminated in frequent bouts of bloodshed. Pro slavery transients led violent attacks against abolitionists and anti slavers, who retaliated in kind. In one particularly brutal incident, the town of Lawrence, Kansas, was "sacked"—the sheriff of the Territorial government led a group of armed men in an attack that burned down the offices of abolitionist newspapers, as well as a hotel and the home of the leader of the Free State government. Abolitionist John Brown, who later led the famous Harper's Ferry raid in Virginia, had come to Kansas to assist in the efforts of the Free State government, and when he heard of the attack on Lawrence, he led a Free State militia in the direction of the town to fight the Territorial militia. He was too late, however, and instead of fighting the militia, he and his men went to the homes of pro slavery men who lived near Pottawatomie Creek, Kansas—some of whom had been slave catchers after the passage of the Fugitive Slave Act. Brown's men took five prisoners, and killed all of them in the same night. The Pottawatomie Massacre, as it came to be known, was only one of many outbursts of bloodshed that arose as a result of the Kansas-

Nebraska Act. The widespread violence in the territory led to its being known as "Bleeding Kansas."

Some years later, when Brown was facing execution for organizing the Harper's Ferry raid, Mahala Doyle, whose husband and two sons were killed by Brown during the Pottawatomie incident, wrote him the following letter:

"Altho vengence is not mine, I confess, that I do feel gratified to hear that you ware stopt in your fiendish career at Harper's Ferry, with the loss of your two sons, you can now appreciate my distress, in Kansas, when you then and there entered my house at midnight and arrested my husband and two boys and took them out of the yard and in cold blood shot them dead in my hearing, you cant say you done it to free our slaves, we had none and never expected to own one, but has only made me a poor disconsolate widow with helpless children while I feel for your folly. I do hope & trust that you will meet your just reward. O how it pained my Heart to hear the dying groans of my Husband and children if this scrawl give you any consolation you are welcome to it. NB, my son John Doyle whose life I begged of you is now grown up and is very desirous to be at Charleston on the day of your execution would certainly be there if his means would permit it, that he might adjust the rope around your neck if governor wise would permit it."

The violence sparked by the issue of slavery was not confined to Kansas, however, nor did it occur solely between the rough and ready militia men of the frontier territories. In May of 1856, after giving a speech that denounced the Kansas-Nebraska Act and blamed people like Stephen A. Douglas for the Bleeding Kansas phenomenon, Senator Charles Sumner was violently attacked and beaten with a cane by Preston Brooks, who was a Congressman in the House of Representatives, and a cousin of Andrew Butler, the other pro slavery senator whom Sumner had targeted in his speech. Debates around slavery had grown particularly uncivilized by this time, even in the United States Congress. Abolitionists and slave owners alike claimed that their views were justified by the Christian religion; abolitionists claimed the contrary, and furthermore, accused slave owners of having sexual relations with their female slaves. Slavery supporters countered with the assertion that abolitionists were advocates for interracial marriage. The unsavory subtext of Sumner's speech alluded to the slave-rape accusations, and for this reason Brooks felt that his family's honor had been impeached.

Reportedly, Brooks initially intended to challenge Sumner to a duel, but decided that Sumner did not deserve the respect inherent in a formal challenge and was instead only worthy of a beating. Brooks attacked Sumner on the floor of the Senate chamber, beating him with his walking stick so severely that Sumner lost consciousness and suffered symptoms of traumatic brain injury for the rest of his life. In the north, the incident was viewed as symbolic of the south's inability to tolerate any challenge to their point of view, and their willingness to violate free speech and open debate. In the south, Brooks' action was considered an act of heroism, revenge for the insults that northern politicians had been laying at the door of the south for years. The attack was taken by many as a sign that it was no longer possible to have a meaningful national dialogue around the issue of slavery—and that war, or some other equally disastrous consequence, was inevitable.

The Dred Scott Decision

"A free negro of the African race, whose ancestors were brought to this country and sold as slaves, is not a "citizen" within the meaning of the Constitution of the United States.

"When the Constitution was adopted, they were not regarded in any of the States as members of the community which constituted the State, and were not numbered among its "people or citizens." Consequently, the special rights and immunities guaranteed to citizens do not apply to them. And not being "citizens" within the meaning of the Constitution, they are not entitled to sue in that character in a court of the United States, and the Circuit Court has not jurisdiction in such a suit[...]

"The change in public opinion and feeling in relation to the African race which has taken place since the adoption of the Constitution cannot change its construction and meaning, and it must be construed and administered now according to its true meaning and intention when it was formed and adopted."

Excerpt from Supreme Court decision on
Scott v. Sanford, 1857

One of the most famous decisions handed down
by the United States Supreme Court, not just
before the war but in all of its history, was the
verdict in the 1857 case of *Dred Scott v. Sanford*.
Scott, a slave, had brought suit against his
owners for his freedom. Scott had been born in
Virginia, and had been a slave his whole life, but
as an adult he had been sold to an army doctor
named John Emerson, and he had accompanied
Emerson to Illinois, which was a free state. The
precedent in American law up to that point held
that slaves became free once they set foot in a
state or territory where slavery was illegal. For
unspecified reasons, however, Scott had not
claimed his freedom while in Illinois, but had
elected to remain with Emerson for many years,
ultimately marrying and having a child while in
Emerson's service. It was not until after
Emerson's death that Scott attempted to

purchase his and his family's freedom from Emerson's widow, who had inherited ownership of them. She refused to allow the purchase, and Scott began to pursue the matter in court, arguing that because of the long period of his residency in free territories, he should have been freed years ago. Interestingly, Scott's legal fees were paid for by the family of Peter Blow, the man who had been Scott's first owner.

After a protracted legal battle in the Missouri lower courts, Scott's suit against the brother of Emerson's widow, John Sanford, to whom ownership of Scott had been transferred, was heard by the Supreme Court. The court returned a holding that stunned the country and outraged nearly everyone who was not an adamant supporter of slavery: because Scott was black, the Court declared that he was not and could never be a citizen of the United States, and therefore he had no standing to bring suit in a court of law. Furthermore, it held that the

Missouri Compromise was unconstitutional and that the federal government had no legal authority to ban slavery anywhere save in the original thirteen states, i.e., the states that existed at the time the Constitution was ratified. It also held that the federal government had no authority to free slaves merely because they had been transported into the free territories.

The Dred Scott ruling frightened and outraged many who had not previously been especially opposed to slavery. In ruling that the government of the United States had no power to illegalize slavery in the territories, the Supreme Court had also effectively nullified the doctrine of popular sovereignty, the cherished cause of northern Democrats such as Stephen A. Douglas. Popular sovereignty held that the residents of the western territories should have the right to vote for or against the legalization of slavery in their own region; the *Scott v. Sanford* ruling, however, meant that even if the residents of a territory such as Kansas voted to exclude slavery, the federal government would not be able to enforce the decision. Northerners opposed to slavery saw this as the end of any possibility of limiting the spread of slavery throughout the country. Southerners who supported slavery used the abolitionist opposition to the ruling as an opportunity to depict them as defying the rule of law.

This legal implication alarmed not only hard line abolitionists, but Free Soil party members, who were generally supportive of slavery and the rights of slave owners, so long as slavery was confined to the south. They opposed the spread of slavery into the western territories, fearing that slave owners would buy up the most fertile farmland and profit from the free labor of their slaves, while non slave owning whites would be unable to make profitable land purchases or compete within the slave economy. The uncertainty that the Dred Scott decision introduced regarding the slavery issue in the western territories provoked a financial crisis, known as the Panic of 1857; financial speculators who had invested in the growing western frontier saw the markets reacting to the fact that no one could now tell whether Kansas and other territories would be slave or free, an uncertainty which impacted the building of railroads, the settlement of white families, and the stability of western banks which had depended on both the railroads and the settlers.

Chief Justice of the Supreme Court Roger Taney, who authored the majority opinion in the Dred Scott case, supposedly believed that the court's ruling would lessen the national division over slavery by leaving nothing for the politicians to debate. The effect was unfortunately the opposite of what he intended: southern Democrats, emboldened by what they saw as a confirmation of their natural and moral right to spread the practice of slavery throughout the country, became even less tolerant of Republican and abolitionist opposition, and more entrenched in the path to secession.

John Brown's Raid on Harper's Ferry

"Old John Brown's body lies moldering in the grave,

While weep the sons of bondage whom he ventured all to save;

But tho he lost his life while struggling for the slave,

His soul is marching on."

Lyrics from the traditional song "John Brown" by William W. Patton

In October of 1859, John Brown, who had led the Free State militia in killing five men during the Pottawatomie Massacre in Kansas several years before, led another armed raid, this time in Harper's Ferry, Virginia. Brown was an extreme abolitionist who believed that slavery would only be ended through a massive armed revolt of slaves, free blacks, and white abolitionists. He intended to incite just such a revolt by attacking and seizing a federal military arsenal, the weapons of which would supply his twenty-man company during a protracted stand-off against the U.S. army. Brown believed that as word of the stand-off spread, slaves, free blacks, and even whites, would flock to Harper's Ferry, and eventually their numbers would be so great as to constitute a small army, which would travel through Virginia and Tennessee, terrifying slave owners and attracting more escaped slaves as members. While Brown and his men succeeded in capturing the armory at first, word had not reached the slaves in the nearby plantations of the revolt and its intentions, so none came to join the fight. Nonetheless, Brown led a raid against a nearby plantation, which belonged to Lewis Washington, the great-grandnephew of George Washington. Lewis Washington, his family, and a number of his slaves were taken hostage.

President James Buchanan ordered a nearby detachment of Marines to capture Brown and his men, and future Confederate general Robert E. Lee, who was home on furlough from Texas, was given command of it. Lee offered Brown a chance to surrender on the condition that his life and the lives of his men would be spared, but Brown refused. Lee ordered the door of the engine house where Brown had barricaded himself broken down, using a ladder as a battering ram. Brown was grievously wounded by a blow from a sword shortly afterward, and his surviving men were arrested. John Brown was tried and hanged on December 2, 1859.

Many abolitionists in the north were appalled by what they termed the "insanity" of Brown's actions. Brown had attempted to enlist both Frederick Douglass and Harriet Tubman in the raid, but Douglass saw the impossibility of the raid succeeding, and warned that Brown was going on a suicide mission. Tubman, on the other hand, was highly in favor of the raid, and intended to participate, but she became ill and was unable to travel to Virginia in time. Eventually, Brown's abolitionist colleagues began to write in support of his actions, claiming that his cause was righteous. Southerners were enraged by this display of approval, and it added to their conviction that abolitionists would stop at nothing to destroy their slave-owning way of life.

The terror that southern slave owners felt at the prospect of a slave uprising was channeled into harsh retaliation nationwide against outspoken abolitionists who lived outside the protection of the most populous free states in the east. This, however, was nothing new.

Some years before the Harper's Ferry raid, in 1837, an abolitionist and Presbyterian minister named Elijah P. Lovejoy was shot and killed at the age of 34 by a pro slavery mob. The mob also destroyed Lovejoy's printing presses by throwing them into the river; it was the third time a mob had destroyed Lovejoy's printing presses. He had left Missouri in the hopes that he could publish his newspaper freely in a non slave state like Illinois. Another resident of Illinois took notice of Lovejoy's violent death, and though he was not an abolitionist himself, he was anti-slavery, and vehemently opposed to any form of mob violence that short-changed the right to free speech. His name was Abraham Lincoln, and Lovejoy's death, as well as the growing national trend towards mob violence, particularly on the part of the pro slavers, angered him deeply. (He coined the term "mobocracy" to refer to the practice of silencing political opponents by intimidation and threats of lynching.) Lovejoy's death became the focus for the speech that launched Lincoln's early career, just after he had been elected to the Illinois General Assembly and admitted to the bar. The issue of slavery would come to define

Lincoln's legal and political career, and later, his presidency.

Chapter Two: War On the Horizon

Abraham Lincoln

Abraham Lincoln, sixteenth president of the United States, is inextricable from any discussion of the Civil War, not merely because he served as president of the Union during the entire course of the conflict, but because he was, arguably, at least partially responsible for starting it.

Lincoln ran as the nominee of the Republican party in the 1860 presidential election against candidates from three other parties, including his old political rival and the author of the Kansas-Nebraska act, Stephen A. Douglas. The debate around slavery had by this time risen to such a fever pitch that South Carolina announced that it would secede from the Union in the case of a Republican presidential victory. South Carolina made good on its promise and announced its secession on December 20, 1860, about a month after the election, but four months before Lincoln was inaugurated. Six states followed South Carolina's example in January and February of 1861, and the final four states to join the Confederacy did so during the spring and summer of that year.

Secession was something of a hysterical over-reaction on the part of South Carolina, as Lincoln had no interest (at least, at the beginning of his term) in attempting to eliminate slavery in the south without the consent of southern voters. He was accused in southern newspapers of being an abolitionist, but Lincoln himself observed mildly that he was not opposed to slavery, merely to the expansion of it—a fairly moderate view that placed him at the center of the Republican party. Indeed, when Lincoln was first elected, the Radical Republican faction, which favored immediate and total abolition of slavery, considered Lincoln too backwards and conservative for their taste. In his first inaugural speech, Lincoln directly addresses the fears of southerners that he intended to abolish slavery:

"Apprehension seems to exist among the people of the Southern States that by the accession of a Republican Administration their property and their peace and personal security are to be endangered. There has never been any reasonable cause for such apprehension. Indeed, the most ample evidence to the contrary has all the while existed and been open to their inspection. It is found in nearly all the published speeches of him who now addresses you. I do but quote from one of those speeches when I declare that—

'I have no purpose, directly or indirectly, to interfere with the institution of slavery in the States where it exists. I believe I have no lawful right to do so, and I have no inclination to do so.'

"Those who nominated and elected me did so with full knowledge that I had made this and many similar declarations and had never recanted them..."

This reassurance did not have the desire effect, however; the southern belief that Lincoln was a devoted abolitionist was too widespread.

Abraham Lincoln was one of the "new men" of the post-Revolutionary War generation in America. He was born on the western frontier, in Kentucky, and he lived in Illinois for almost his entire adult life. Lincoln had survived a miserably impoverished backwoods upbringing under the tyrannical rule of a shiftless father, who hired Lincoln out like an indentured servant to work on farms and on river boats, collecting all of Lincoln's wages for his own use. Lincoln worked for his father's benefit between the ages of sixteen and twenty-one, a period of life during which most young men would have been pursuing a career or an education. Lincoln, however, was an enthusiastic autodidact who gleaned as much knowledge as he could possibly extract from books he had borrowed or rented from neighbors.

After Lincoln became a legal adult at the age of twenty-one, his family moved to Indiana, and Lincoln parted ways with them. He worked various jobs, first as a waterman on the river, then in the small Illinois town of New Salem, where, in his twenties, he served as a postmaster and a clerk in a general store. Lincoln studied law in his spare time, reading dense legal tomes which he had to save up for and purchase one by one. Eventually, he passed the bar exam without having attended law school or even having undertaken the usual term of apprenticeship to an older lawyer, which was how many young frontier lawyers got their training.

In addition to practicing law, Lincoln served a number of years as a legislator in the Illinois General Assembly, where his principle political agenda was attempting to link the scattered frontier settlements in the less populated areas of Illinois with the major cities and with each other, via public works projects such as roads, bridges, and railroads. After he left the General Assembly, he served a single term as an Illinois state representative in Congress, before returning to Springfield to practice law. As a member of Congress, he called into question President James K. Polk's actions during the Mexican-American War, all but accusing Polk of having provoked the conflict by deliberately marching American soldiers into a contested territory where the Mexicans would be certain to fire on them. Lincoln's opposition to the Mexican-American War made him deeply unpopular back in Illinois, where the war was popular, and when his Congressional term came to an end, Lincoln returned to Springfield to practice law, doubtful whether he would ever again return to political life.

Lincoln's political renaissance was sparked by Stephen A. Douglas introducing the Kansas-Nebraska Act and popular sovereignty to Congress. Lincoln was among those who found the de facto overturn of the Missouri Compromise an outrageous over-reach by the slave powers. As a result, Lincoln became one of the principle members of the Whig party in Illinois involved in organizing the new Republican party around the anti slavery agenda. Despite his stint in the United States Congress, Lincoln was not nationally famous; however, in Springfield and in Illinois political circles, he was known to be an excellent speaker, witty and entertaining, interspersing his political talks and law lectures with humorous, sometimes ribald anecdotes.

Lincoln's rise to national prominence came 1858, when he ran against Stephen A. Douglas for the Illinois Senate seat. Douglas had held the Senate seat for a number of years, but the Kansas-Nebraska Act, and the rippling consequences of popular sovereignty, had led to a split in the Democratic party, with Southern Democrats forming their own platform. Douglas was a famous public speaker, and Lincoln challenged him to participate in joint debates before the public, in each of Illinois' voting districts. Douglas agreed only reluctantly. The debates all centered around the issue of slavery. Lincoln lost the Senate race by a slim margin, but after publishing his debate speeches in book form, he became nationally famous, and a viable candidate for the Republican party presidential nomination.

As previously mentioned, Lincoln's views on slavery were not extreme. He was a canny, skilled politician who made shrewd distinctions between his personal views and opinions, and his agendas and goals as a public man and elected official. He was not an abolitionist; he had a strong regard for property rights, and could not support the agenda of slavery being abolished without compensation for slave owners. He possessed an even stronger belief in rule by consent of the governed—he would not support any measure that called for slavery to be abolished without the participating votes of slave owners. But Lincoln had a deep personal desire to see slavery ended in his lifetime, as became evident once he became president. He often expressed public irritation with abolitionists, claiming that they exacerbated the suffering of slaves to a greater degree than even the pro slavery faction. Lincoln believed that the intense emotions surrounding the slavery debate were an obstacle to making any kind of progress on the slavery issue itself. He felt that abolitionists who called for the immediate and total end of slavery only aggravated southern fears of slave rebellions, and that by issuing insults against slave owners, abolitionists only entrenched southern resistance to political dialogue with the north.

Lincoln's centrist views on slavery aligned him with the majority of the Republican party, especially in the west; abolitionists were a decided minority, concentrated primarily in New England. This played an important role in helping Lincoln secure the Republican party's nomination for the presidential election of 1860.

The Election of 1860

"I was in the East when that Cooper Institute speech was delivered. Have you ever watched the turning of the tide – a slow, resistless motion in one direction and a moment later a slow resistless motion in another? That was what you could see in the East as the result of that speech. Men said as they read it: 'Well, what? Who is this? Here is a strong man – a man of grasp and force. Why, this man would do for the Presidency.'"

> Charles Caverno, referring to Lincoln's famous speech at the Cooper Union

Lincoln was by no means the obvious or overwhelming favorite choice to receive the Republican nomination. In fact, it was generally assumed that New York Senator William H. Seward (whom Lincoln would later appoint as his Secretary of State) had secured the nomination well in advance. However, Seward had alienated important allies within the party, and Lincoln's campaign manager was busily converting every voter who did not absolutely support Seward into a supporter for Lincoln. When Lincoln received the Republican nomination, it was generally assumed to be because the party leaders could not all agree on their first choice of candidate, but that they had been united on Lincoln as their second choice.

Four political parties presented candidates during the 1860 election: Lincoln represented the new Republican party, and his chief opponent, John C. Breckenridge of Kentucky, represented the new Southern Democratic party. The Democratic party, which had split over the issue of popular sovereignty, fielded Stephen A. Douglas as their candidate, while the new Constitutional Union party (also known as the Bell-Everett party) nominated John Bell of Tennessee. (The Constitutional Union party was primarily composed of former Whigs who were generally anti slavery, but who were more concerned with mollifying the southern states so that they would not secede.)

The election of 1860 exposed the sectional lines dividing the country. Breckenridge carried almost all of the south, from North Carolina to Florida to as far west as Texas; he also carried the border states of Maryland and Delaware.

(Not a single elector from below the Missouri Compromise line voted for Lincoln.) Lincoln himself carried all of New England and much of what is now considered the Mid-west, as well as western states such as California and Oregon. John Bell of the Constitutional Union party won the border states of Virginia, Tennessee, and Kentucky. Stephen A. Douglas carried only the slave state of Missouri, but the tally of the popular vote put him second in the race, behind Lincoln. Douglas also the only candidate to win votes from electors from both slave and free states; elsewhere the election was divided strictly along slavery and secession lines.

The voter turnout for the election of 1860 was, at the time, higher than in any other election in the nation's history; since then, the record has only been broken once, in 1876. This is both a reflection of the multiplicity of views represented by the four parties, and of the intensity of feeling that existed over the issue of slavery in the mid nineteenth century.

Secession Begins: South Carolina

Secession rhetoric had played a role in South Carolina politics since the 1830's, but in the run up to the election of 1860, calls for secession in the South Carolina General Assembly did not meet with the tempering or moderating influence that southern Whigs had once imparted to the debate. The parties had broken along sectional lines, and southerners voted as southerners, not as Democrats or Republicans. Calls for South Carolina's secession began early in the year, and on November 9, 1860, within just a few days of the election results being made known to the public, the South Carolina General Assembly passed the "Resolution to Call the Election of Abraham Lincoln as U.S. President a Hostile Act". A special convention session was called for, and by late December of 1860 the South Carolina legislature had passed an ordinance, entitled "A Declaration of the

Immediate Causes Which May Induce and Justify the Secession of South Carolina from the Federal Union". It made reference to previous secession debates and explained why South Carolina had not seceded at the time, and why it was seceding now, as demonstrated in the excerpt quoted below:

"But an increasing hostility on the part of the non-slaveholding States to the institution of slavery, has led to a disregard of their obligations, and the laws of the General Government have ceased to effect the objects of the Constitution. The States of Maine, New Hampshire, Vermont, Massachusetts, Connecticut, Rhode Island, New York, Pennsylvania, Illinois, Indiana, Michigan, Wisconsin and Iowa, have enacted laws which either nullify the Acts of Congress or render useless any attempt to execute them. In many of these States the fugitive is discharged from service or labor claimed, and in none of them has the State Government complied with the stipulation made in the Constitution. The State of New Jersey, at an early day, passed a law in conformity with her constitutional obligation; but the current of anti-slavery feeling has led her more recently to enact laws which render inoperative the remedies provided by her own law and by the laws of Congress. In the State of New York even the right of transit for a slave has been denied by her tribunals; and the States of Ohio and Iowa have refused to surrender to justice fugitives charged with murder, and with inciting servile insurrection in the State of Virginia."

It was widely believed in the south that Republicans in general, and Abraham Lincoln in particular, were in favor of giving black men equal civil rights to white men, including full citizenship and the right to vote. More damningly, they ascribed to Lincoln a full belief in complete racial equality—the idea that blacks and whites are born with equal mental, intellectual, spiritual, and moral potential. This was not, in fact, the case; Lincoln did not believe in racial equality, and while towards the end of his life he was beginning to hint at the possibility of giving black men the right to vote, this was not until after the Thirteenth Amendment had been passed and the Civil War had come to a close. He never made any efforts along those lines while he was president. But Lincoln did oppose the spread of slavery from outside the south into the western territories, and that alone was reason enough to secede in the minds of most South Carolinians. Unless slavery expanded, they reasoned, it would eventually die off, even within the south, and with it an entire society and way of life would be lost. White southerners could not be white southerners unless blacks were slaves. This is why, when historians speak of the South fighting to "preserve" slavery, it would be more accurate to say that the South fought to *spread* slavery.

By March of 1860, shortly before Abraham Lincoln's first presidential inauguration, seven states became signatories to the Confederate Constitution. James Buchanan, the outgoing president, considered the secession to be illegal, but he also considered the use of the U.S. army to prevent secession unconstitutional; effectively, he left the situation unresolved for Lincoln to deal with. South Carolina, as we discussed earlier, seceded on the 20th of December in 1860. Between January ninth and February first of 1861, Mississippi, Florida, Alabama, Georgia, Louisiana, and Texas also seceded, and in that order. The last four states to join the Confederacy did not do so until after the war had started, and Lincoln had called for volunteer militias from the Union states to take up arms against the South. Virginia seceded in April of 1861, Arkansas and North Carolina in May, and Tennessee in June. In Kentucky, a secession ordinance was passed, but not acted upon;

Kentucky remained part of the Union, but fielded a number of volunteers for the Confederate army. Missouri likewise passed a secession ordinance, but did not present it to Missouri voters for ratification.

Lincoln was adamantly opposed to secession. As we discussed earlier, there was some division of feeling as to whether or not the individual states of the Union had the right to dissolve political ties and become independent. In the "Declaration of Immediate Causes" ordinance, the authors refer to the treaty made between the United States and Great Britain after the Revolution, which refers to the states as "free, sovereign, and independent", and affirms that the states had functioned in the past, and could easily function in the future, as disparate and independent countries.

Lincoln, however, considered it his principle duty to hold the Union together. He once remarked to a Republican colleague, "We say to the southern disunionists, we won't go out of the Union, and you shan't." To Lincoln, the rebellion of the southern states was merely a refusal by the minority to abide by the ruling of the majority—and the rule of a majority vote is the principal basis for the rule of law. But Lincoln's strongest argument against secession lay in his interpretation of Section IV, Article IV of the Constitution, reproduced below:

"The United States shall guarantee to every state in this union a republican form of government, and shall protect each of them against invasion; and on application of the legislature, or of the executive (when the legislature cannot be convened) against domestic violence."

Lincoln interpreted this section of the Constitution to mean that the federal government was required to preserve a republican government in every state, even if the state's political leaders claimed that it no longer wished for such.

The Firing on Fort Sumter

For about three months after South Carolina announced its secession from the Union, hostilities were at a stand still. Although the federal government did not recognize South Carolina's independence, Lincoln was reluctant to take military action against Americans if he did not absolutely have to. It was the decision taken by South Carolina to escalate hostilities between themselves and the Union that led to the first shots of the Civil War being fired.

All military bases in the United States are the property of the federal government, rather than the states in which they reside. This placed the

American soldiers stationed in South Carolina in a great predicament; some were South Carolina born, and loyal to the South, while others were from the north or the west and loyal to the Union. South Carolina was already gathering men and weapons for what would eventually be the Confederate army; it viewed the fortifications and weapons belonging to U.S. army bases as the property of the newly declared independent republic.

One of these contested U.S. army bases was Fort Sumter, located on a tiny island in the harbor of Charleston, which was one of the South's most crucial port cities. Fort Sumter was strategically crucial; it sat just in the middle of the harbor, commanding a 360 degree view of surrounding land and water, and had been specially designed to rival the defense capabilities of any military out-posting in the world. On December 24, 1860, just two days after South Carolina declared secession, Major Robert Anderson, the officer in command of nearby Fort Moultrie, abandoned his post in the middle of the night and stealthily transferred the men under his command to Fort Sumter. Fort Moultrie was not especially valuable—the South Carolinians hadn't even bothered to secure it—but the secessionists would not be safe in Charleston unless they controlled Fort Sumter.

For about three months, Fort Sumter was the last remaining federal outpost in South Carolina. By the time Lincoln took office on March 4, 1861, the Union soldiers at Fort Sumter were in desperate need of being re-supplied by a Union ship. However, South Carolina had sent picket ships to patrol the waters around the fort. (In the famous *Star of the West* incident, cadets from the South Carolina military academy, The Citadel, fired on a ship attempting to transport supplies to Fort Sumter; these were technically the first shots fired in the Civil War, but Union forces did not retaliate, possibly due to the fact that the cadets were only students.)

Attempts at re-supply had been ongoing during the last two months of James Buchanan's term. Almost as soon as Lincoln took office, he was informed that Anderson's men had only another six weeks' worth of supplies before they would have no choice but to surrender. Lincoln sent word to the governor of South Carolina, Francis W. Pickins, that he intended to dispatch a relief ship to Charleston harbor. The response of Pickins and the South Carolina provisional government was to demand that Anderson and his men evacuate the fort and surrender it to Confederate solders. There was some talk of South Carolina purchasing federal lands in the state under the terms of a peace treaty with the United States, but it was impossible for the Union to enter into a treaty with a state that it regarded as mounting an illegal rebellion. Anderson offered to surrender before shots were fired at all, but he and Beauregard were unable to settle on terms for a truce.

Confederate forces soon began to fire on Fort Sumter from nearby Fort Johnson, but Anderson did not return fire until daylight. After exchanging fire for two days, Beauregard offered Anderson the opportunity to evacuate his starving and exhausted men from the fort without surrendering; accordingly, at 2 PM on April 14, 1861, Anderson and his men were conveyed to the Union relief ship that had been unable to reach them earlier. Thus, the first battle of the Civil War ended with no casualties.

Now that Confederate soldiers had fired upon Union soldiers, Lincoln wasted no further time in waging open war. He sent out a presidential proclamation calling for seventy five thousand volunteers to swell the ranks of the Union army, with quotas for individual states. Some states responded enthusiastically to the call for volunteers, while reactions were more conflicted in the border states, where slavery was legal but secession was unpopular.

Near the end of Civil War, Lincoln commented on this first outbreak of hostilities: "Both parties deprecated war, but one of them would make war rather than let the nation survive, and the other would accept war rather than let it perish, and the war came."

Early Days of the Civil War

Not every slave state seceded and joined the Confederacy. The areas of the upper south and Midwest which had voted overwhelmingly for the Constitutional Unionist party during the recent presidential election hosted voters who tended to support slavery but oppose secession. The result was a peculiar kind of tension regarding whether the so called "border states" would eventually decide to join the Confederacy after all, or whether they would remain loyal to the Union.

On March 2, 1861, two days before Abraham Lincoln was inaugurated as president, one of Lincoln's erstwhile rivals for the Republican nomination, William H. Seward, the senator from New York, proposed a new amendment to the Constitution. He was joined in his efforts by Congressman Thomas Corwin of Ohio, who brought the amendment before the House of Representatives; as a result, it is now known as the Corwin Amendment. The goal of the Corwin Amendment was to persuade the seceding southern states to return to the Union. The amendment would illegalize any effort by the federal government to disband what the amendment referred to as "domestic institutions"—a coded reference to slavery, which was often referred to as the "peculiar institution". Below is the full text of the amendment as it was presented to the Senate:

"No amendment shall be made to the Constitution which will authorize or give to Congress the power to abolish or interfere, within any State, with the domestic institutions thereof, including that of persons held to labor or service by the laws of said State."

The version of the amendment which was presented to the House was altered, but fundamentally similar in scope.

Had the Corwin Amendment been passed, it would have been the Thirteenth Amendment to the United States Constitution—and the Thirteenth Amendment as we know it could not have been made into law unless it first specifically repealed the previous amendment. (Passing an amendment solely to repeal a previous amendment has only been done once in American constitutional history: the Eighteenth

Amendment, which prohibited the sale of alcohol in the United States, was repealed by the Twenty-First Amendment.)

The goal of the Corwin Amendment was to entice the seceding southern states back to the Union— and even if that should fail, to give reassurance to the border states, all of which were slave states, that their interests would be looked after if they continued to be loyal to the Union.

The Corwin Amendment passed by simple majority vote in both houses of Congress, and was signed by President James Buchanan two days before his term expired; the presidential signature is not required on Constitutional amendments, so Buchanan's gesture was merely one of approval and solidarity. The amendment was not yet law, however. Constitution amendments must be passed with a two thirds Congressional majority to take effect, and owing to the secession of the southern states (and the consequent withdrawal of their senators and representatives) a two thirds majority was not possible.

Thus, the amendment was passed to the state legislatures for ratification, but by that time the war had begun, and popular feeling about the south had changed somewhat. It was initially believed that only a handful of southerners, mostly politicians, were in favor of secession, and that once fighting had begun, thousands of southerners who were secretly loyal to the Union would emerge and dilute the ranks of the Confederate army. The war had not long progressed, however, before it became apparent that secession had widespread popular support in the south, and that the conflict, which both sides believed would be settled swiftly, would drag on for years. Only Ohio, Maryland, and Illinois ratified the amendment, and in 1864, when it began to be clear that the Union would win the war, the Corwin Amendment was withdrawn from consideration (though, interestingly, it is still technically pending before Congress).

The slave states that chose not to secede from the Union were Maryland and Delaware in the east, and Tennessee and Kentucky further west. The state of Virginia actually split in half over the issue of secession; once Union forces had driven Confederate troops out of the western half of the state, West Virginia formed its own independent state government, which was loyal to the Union. Virginia was one of several states, such as Missouri, Kentucky, and Tennessee, which had dual governments during the war—one Union and one Confederate.

Lincoln's 75,000 Volunteers

On April 15, 1861, shortly after the firing on Ft. Sumter, Lincoln, who had been in office for just over a month, put out a call for 75,000 volunteers to sign up for three months of fighting. There were, at the time, only 14,000 men and 800 officers already serving in the regular army, a number dwarfed by the volunteers flocking to the Confederate army. This was the first time that the United States had expanded its army in such a manner; normally, the state militias made up the bulk of the country's fighting force. In the mid-nineteenth century, owing to the Military Act of 1795, there were strict legal limits regarding the size of the nation's army and the President's ability to expand it—75,000 was the maximum number of soldiers the President was allowed to ask for, and three months was the longest period for which soldiers were allowed to be enlisted. (It is worth mentioning, however, that in 1861, everyone in both the north and in the south believed that the war would be over very quickly—possibly in even less than three months—so the legal limit on enlistments was not initially seen as a hardship.)

Just as Lincoln's election had triggered the secession of the first seven states to join the Confederacy, Lincoln's call for volunteers triggered the secession of the remaining four, states which had been reluctant to secede before the hostilities at Ft. Sumter, but who would not be inclined to furnish the requested regiments to go to war against their near neighbors. Virginia seceded two days after the call for volunteers, on April 17, 1861; its governor, John Letcher, had previously declared that Virginia wished to remain neutral in the conflict, but his state joined the Confederacy when this proved an impossibility.

Arkansas, which was sparsely populated but loyal to its southern neighbors, followed Virginia on May 6. North Carolina, bordered by the Confederate states of Virginia to the north, South Carolina to the south, and the strongly pro-Southern Tennessee to the west, declared secession on May 20, 1861. North Carolina was rich in slaves and plantations in its coastal and central regions, and it possessed one of the Confederacy's largest and most important seaport cities, Wilmington. Its mountainous western region was, like West Virginia, almost devoid of slavery, and its people were mostly loyal to the Union; nonetheless, so many Confederate volunteers emerged from the coastal and central regions of North Carolina that in the end the state furnished more soldiers to the Confederate army than any other. Tennessee followed North Carolina on June 8, 1861. Tennessee's mountainous eastern region was also strongly pro Union, and the secession vote won there by only a narrow margin. Tennessee was the site of more battles fought during the Civil War than any other state besides Virginia, and it was the first Confederate state to be re-captured by the Union.

Reproduced below is the text of Secretary of War William H. Seward's message, sent on Lincoln's orders to the governors of every state that had not already seceded, calling for regiments to make up the quota of volunteers:

"CALL TO ARMS!!

75,000 VOLUNTEERS WANTED

Washington, April 15.

The following is the form of call on the respective state Governors for troops, issued to-day:

"Sir:—Under the act of Congress for calling out the militia to execute the laws of the Union to suppress insurrection, repel invasion, &c., approved February 28th, 1795, I have the honor to request your Excellency to cause to be immediately detached from the militia of your state, the quota designated in the table below to serve as infantry or riflemen for three months, or sooner, if discharged.

"Your Excellancy will please communicate to me the time about which your quota will be expected at its rendezvous, as it will be met as soon as possible by an officer or officers to muster it into the service and pay of the United States; at the same time the oath of fidelity to the United States will be administrated to every officer and man. The mustering officers will be instructed to receive no man under the rank of commissioned officer who is apparently over 45 or under 18 years, or who is not in physical strength and vigor. The quota to each state is as follows: Maine, New Hampshire, Vermont, Rhode Island, Connecticut, Delaware, Arkansas, Michigan, Wisconsin, Iowa, and Minnesota, one regiment each; New York 17 regiments; Pennsylvania, 15 regiments; Ohio, 13; New Jersey, Maryland, Kentucky, Missouri, four regiments each; Illinois and Indiana, six regiments each; Virginia, three regiments.

"It is ordered that each regiment shall consist of an aggregate of officers and men of 1,780 men.

"The total thus to be called out is 73,910 men, the remainder, which constitutes the 75,000 under the President's proclamation will be composed of troops in the District of Columbia."

The reply of Virginia governor John Letcher spoke not only for the border states that were shortly to join the Confederacy, but for the south generally:

"In reply to this communication, I have only to say that the militia of Virginia will not be furnished to the powers at Washington for any such use or purpose as they have in view. Your object is to subjugate the Southern States, and a requisition made upon me for such an object -- an object, in my judgment, not within the purview of the Constitution or the act of 1795 --

will not be complied with. You have chosen to inaugurate civil war, and having done so, we will meet it in a spirit as determined as the Administration has exhibited towards the South."

Chapter Three: The Civil War Begins

Jefferson Davis, President of the Confederate States of America

Abraham Lincoln's southern counterpart was Jefferson Davis, a graduate of the prestigious American military academy of West Point, who had served as a Senator from Mississippi for a number of years and was U.S. Secretary of War under President Franklin Pierce. Davis was among the delegates who attended the Nashville Convention in 1850; dissatisfied with the moderate, unionist outcome of the convention, Davis helped organize a second gathering of the convention, which was attended only by his fellow radical secessionists. Jefferson Davis was among the South's strongest and most vocal advocates for the "positive good" theory of slavery—that is, the belief that slavery was more than evil to be tolerated for pragmatic reasons, but rather a divinely appointed institution of white supremacy over the "African race".

Davis was born in Kentucky, but moved at an early age to Mississippi, where his family owned a cotton plantation. He was educated at Transylvania University, in Lexington, Kentucky, among other institutions, including West Point; following his graduation from the military academy, he joined one of the traditional regiments of the American army that had been founded during the Revolutionary War. Like Abraham Lincoln, he served briefly during the Black Hawk War against the Sauk, Meskwakis, and Kickapoos tribes in the western frontier. Davis was briefly married to Sarah Taylor, whose father, Zachary Taylor, would later be elected president, but the marriage ended when Taylor died of malaria three months after the wedding. Davis had resigned his commission at the time of his marriage, and after his wife's death he returned to his family's plantation, where he acquired more than a hundred slaves. For several years, he was a recluse who spent most of his time riding on horseback along the borders of his property and scouting the woods nearby; he also spent a great deal of time engaged in the quiet study of books in his home.

Davis entered politics in 1840, and ran unsuccessfully for a seat in the House of Representatives in 1843; he ran again and was elected in 1845. In 1841, he met and married his second wife, Varina Howell; Davis was thirty five at the time, and Howell seventeen. When the Mexican-American War began in 1846, Davis resigned his seat in the House of Representatives to serve as a volunteer officer—unlike Lincoln, who used his position in Congress to protest the war. Curiously, one of Davis's chief interests during the time he spent as an elected official in Washington was the building project that produced the American Capitol building. The Congressional chambers in use during the nineteenth century were small, cramped, and had poor acoustics, which made it almost impossible for Congressmen giving speeches to make themselves heard past the front row. As new states entered the union, the need for a larger, more capably designed building was evident, and Davis committed himself to the project throughout his two senate terms and his tenure in Franklin Pierce's cabinet.

Davis's politics followed the trajectory of the south in general during the decades leading to the Civil War. In 1847 the governor of Mississippi appointed him to fill a senate seat which had been left vacant by the previous occupant's death. Davis, an ardent advocate for the expansion of slavery, joined other southern politicians in attempting to introduce slavery into the territories newly acquired from Mexico. Three years later, angered by the anti-slavery provisions of the Compromise of 1850, Davis resigned his senate seat to run for governor of

Mississippi. He was not elected, but after he assisted fellow Democrat Franklin Pierce in successfully campaigning for the presidency, Pierce appointed him Secretary of War. Pierce lost the Democratic nomination to James Buchanan after only his first term in office, and Davis returned to the Senate, where he served until Mississippi announced its secession from the Union on January 9, 1861. A month later, during the first and only Confederate constitutional convention, he was elected president of the Confederacy, due largely to his reputation for championing slavery throughout his career in Washington, as well as his considerable military expertise—as the former Secretary of War, Davis knew better than anyone else in the South what the Confederate army would be facing if there was war with the Union.

In June of 1862, a year and a half after the Civil War began, Davis appointed fellow West Point graduate and Mexican-American War veteran

Robert E. Lee commander of the Confederate Army of Northern Virginia, replacing the wounded Joseph E. Johnston. The South won a number of strategic victories early in the war, but also suffered from mismanagement, as when Generals Johnston and Pierre Beauregard failed to pursue the retreating Union army after they were defeated at the Battle of Bull Run.

Robert E. Lee

Robert E. Lee was the son of a famous father— "Light Horse Harry" Lee, an officer in the Revolutionary War—who died when his son was eleven. Lee grew up with his five brothers and sisters under the care of his mother, Anne, who died shortly after Lee returned home after finishing his education at West Point. When he was twenty four, Lee married Mary Custis, the great-granddaughter of Martha Custis Washington, wife of George Washington. In marrying Custis, Lee curiously found himself in the same position as the nation's first president when it came to the management of the famous

Custis estate. When Mary Custis's father died, Lee was made the executor of his will. Custis had ordered that his slaves be freed within five years of his death, but Lee, upon discovering that the estate had been badly mismanaged and was losing money, decided that he must postpone the emancipation for as long as possible. This made the slaves angry and discontented, because they had been led to believe that their emancipation would follow immediately after their former master's death. The connection to George Washington lies in the fact that, while Washington ordered his own slaves freed in his will, following the death of his wife, the Custis family slaves his wife had inherited could not legally be freed by him unless he purchased them from the Custis estate. In other words, Lee was charged with freeing the descendants of the same slaves Washington had been legally barred from freeing.

Lee's personal feelings regarding slavery and the Confederacy have been a point of some debate. Lee seems not to have been in favor of secession, but his loyalty to the state of Virginia was such that when Virginia seceded from the Union, his resignation from the U.S. army was inevitable. His views on slavery were somewhat more confused; not unlike George Washington, he viewed slavery as an evil, but nonetheless held the view that it was a divinely appointed institution. He did not hesitate to inflict harsh punishments on his own slaves if they attempted to run away or otherwise flout white authority.

Lee was named a full general of the Confederate army in April of 1861, and his first task was to head the southern forces in West Virginia. There, he suffered a number of defeats and setbacks. His reputation was made, however, when he took command of the Army of Northern Virginia in 1862, beginning a campaign that took the Confederate army as far north as Pennsylvania.

The War Begins: Lincoln's Proclamation of Blockade

On April 19, 1861, Lincoln commanded the first official Union military action of the Civil War: a blockade against the ports in the southern states of South Carolina, Georgia, Alabama, Florida, Louisiana, Mississippi, and Texas. He also ordered the construction of a significant number of ships; the U.S. fleet was approximately 250 vessels strong in 1861, but this number would increase to 600 by the war's end in 1865. The south was heavily dependent on the foreign trade of cotton with nations such as England, and the blockade was thus a severe blow to the Confederacy's economy; it also prevented the movement of troops from one state to the next. Furthermore, the South did not have the manufacturing capacity of the north, and the blockade prevented the shipping of weapons and tools it had been used to receiving from its trading partners. Below is an excerpt from Lincoln's official proclamation of the blockade:

"Now, therefore, I, Abraham Lincoln, President of the United States, with a view to the same purposes before mentioned, and to the protection of the public peace, and the lives and property of quiet and orderly citizens pursuing their lawful occupations, until Congress shall have assembled and deliberated on the said unlawful proceedings, or until the same shall ceased, have further deemed it advisable to set on foot a blockade of the ports within the States aforesaid, in pursuance of the laws of the United States, and of the law of Nations, in such case provided. For this purpose a competent force will be posted so as to prevent entrance and exit of vessels from the ports aforesaid. If, therefore, with a view to violate such blockade, a vessel shall approach, or shall attempt to leave either of the said ports, she will be duly warned by the Commander of one of the blockading vessels, who will endorse on her register the fact and date of such warning, and if the same vessel shall again attempt to enter or leave the blockaded port, she will be captured and sent to the nearest convenient port, for such proceedings against her and her cargo as prize, as may be deemed advisable."

The most interesting legal wrinkle to arise from Lincoln's proclamation of blockade was the fact that, by this order, Lincoln had arguably recognized the Confederacy as an independent sovereign nation, rather than a rebellious faction within the United States. This was of more significance to the Confederacy than to the Union, because the Confederacy was attempting to gain official recognition by foreign nations, England and France in particular, in order to establish treaties and gain allies that would come to its assistance in fighting the Union. From a historical perspective, the blockade was significant because it was held by the U.S. Supreme Court, in later years, as the Union's official declaration of war against the South, despite the fact that scholars and historians generally date the firing on Ft. Sumter as the starting date of the war.

Maintaining the blockade was a monumental effort, because it covered 3500 miles of coast line, stretching along the Atlantic seaboard and into the Gulf of Mexico. At the outbreak of the Civil War, the Confederate navy consisted of a mere 35 vessels, and the naval power of the Union posed a considerable threat to Confederate supply lines. While no foreign nation ever extended official recognition of sovereignty to the Confederacy, England was sufficiently invested in cotton trade with the South to assist in the running of the Union blockade. Blockade runners were fast, maneuverable, light weight ships that delivered supplies to Southern ports by sneaking past Union war ships—"running" the blockade, rather than "breaking" it, which would have required open combat and the defeat of the heavily armed

Union vessels. Southern based trading firms worked with privately owned English and French ships to transport goods from neutral ports in Cuba and elsewhere to deliver goods to Southern ports such as Wilmington and Charleston. An estimate eighty per cent of blockade runs were successful in evading the Union ships and delivering their cargo.

The First Battle of Bull Run

The first major battle of the Civil War—as determined by the number of casualties—was the first Battle of Bull Run. (The battle was referred to by the Confederates as the Battle of Manassas; Union strategists tended to name the site of engagement after natural landmarks such as rivers, while Confederate strategists named them for whichever town or city was closest.) It was not the first armed engagement between Union and Confederate forces; prior to Bull Run there had been a number of minor skirmishes. But as the months wore on, Lincoln felt increasing pressure to take decisive military action that would bring the war to a swift close. The Union army was composed mostly of volunteers who had signed up for the maximum three month enlistment period; by July, Lincoln feared that if the army did not strike immediately, the Union would lose the bulk of its fighting force before the South had been subdued.

The Battle of Bull Run took place on July 21, 1861, just a few miles from Washington D.C. The Confederate army was under the command of General Pierre Beauregard, who had overseen southern troops firing on Ft. Sumter earlier in the year. Beauregard's forces were all that stood between the Union army and the newly instated Confederate capitol of Richmond, Virginia, which was only a short distance from the Union capital of Washington. Believing that a siege on Richmond would crush southern morale and prevent further fighting, Lincoln ordered General Irvin McDowell, the Union commander, to attack. The Confederate and Union armies in the area were more or less equally matched at about 18,000 men. However, both sides were drastically unprepared for battle, and immense losses were the result. There were more than 4,700 casualties, more or less evenly divided between the two sides; the men killed numbered in the hundreds, while thousands of both Union and Confederate soldiers were wounded.

Both McDowell and Beauregard had devised complex battle plans with the goal of flanking the opposing army from the left, but McDowell's plan was too complicated to execute with untried and poorly trained volunteer soldiers. Beauregard's forces were relieved by the arrival of fresh troops under the command of General Joseph E. Johnston, who reached the battle by train in the middle of the day. With these reinforcements, Confederate troops were able to break the right flank of the Union line. Union forces broke into a mass retreat by foot towards the refuge of Washington. Beauregard (and by extension, Confederate president Jefferson Davis) was later criticized for failing to pursue the Union army in retreat, but the Confederate forces were nearly as exhausted and disorganized as their opponents, and were unable to regroup in time for a pursuit. The retreating Union soldiers did not reach Washington for nearly thirty-six hours, arriving limping, exhausted, and in no shape for another immediate fight.

The costliness of Bull Run demonstrated to Lincoln and Union military leadership that there was no possibility of ending the war swiftly. On July 22, 1861, the day after the Battle of Bull Run, Congress authorized a call for 500,000 more volunteers to join the Union army. Furthermore, Lincoln, dissatisfied with McDowell's performance on the battlefield, relieved him of his command and placed Major General George B. McClellan in charge of organizing the new influx of untrained soldiers flooding the Union army; the Army of Northern

Virginia was folded into the new Army of the Potomac. (In November of 1861, after the resignation of General Winfield Scott, McClellan was made general-in-chief of the entire Union army.) On the Confederate side, however, Beauregard was hailed as a hero, despite criticisms that he had not taken full advantage of his victory.

Battle of Antietam

On February 22, 1862—a date which was chosen because it coincided with George Washington's birthday—Abraham Lincoln issued General War Order No. 1, reproduced below:

"Ordered that the 22nd day of February 1862, be the day for a general movement of the Land and Naval forces of the United States against the insurgent forces.

"That especially --

The Army at & about, Fortress Monroe.

The Army of the Potomac.

The Army of Western Virginia

The Army near Munfordsville, Ky.

The Army and Flotilla at Cairo.

And a Naval force in the Gulf of Mexico, be ready for a movement on that day.

"That all other forces, both Land and Naval, with their respective commanders, obey existing orders, for the time, and be ready to obey additional orders when duly given.

"That the Heads of Departments, and especially the Secretaries of War and of the Navy, with all their subordinates; and the General-in-Chief, with all other commanders and subordinates, of Land and Naval forces, will severally be held to their strict and full responsibilities, for the prompt execution of this order."

In issuing this order, Lincoln was shaking off the lethargy that for many months had plagued the

Union army. Lincoln had appointed General George McClellan head of all the Union forces in November of 1861, and McClellan had done a superior job of organizing the masses of Union volunteers into a professional army. However, McClellan was openly contemptuous of Lincoln and his Secretary of War, Edwin Stanton. After being appointed to his position, McClellan wrote to his wife that he was being deferred to by Lincoln and his cabinet and that he had, in effect, become "the real power in the land". Lincoln was a humble person, and he was fully prepared to ignore McClellan's open rudeness, even when he paid a call to McClellan's house to discuss strategy, only to suffer the insult of McClellan's retiring to bed and refusing to see him. But McClellan was also secretive, refusing to fully communicate with Lincoln's staff regarding his plans for the army. Convinced that Lee's Confederate forces outnumbered his own, even when presented with intelligence indicating the contrary, McClellan demonstrated a peculiar reluctant to use the army he had built for its intended purpose. After the first Battle of Bull Run in July, McClellan kept his army out of the fighting for most of the rest of the year.

Frustrated by McClellan's inaction, Lincoln gave command of a large number of his troops to the Army of Virginia under General John Pope. However, Pope narrowly avoided defeat at the second Battle of Bull Run. McClellan was inarguably the more talented and capable commander when he chose to exert himself; furthermore, he had the backing of Union Democrats (and would later run as the Democratic candidate against Lincoln in the presidential election of 1864.) Lincoln therefore had no choice but to give McClellan the opportunity to halt Lee's invasion of Union territory in Maryland. Accordingly, McClellan confronted Lee at the Battle of Antietam (or the Battle of Sharpsburg, in Confederate nomenclature) on September 17, 1862.

The Confederate army, prior to Antietam, had confined themselves to defensive battles, but Lee believed that the strategic gains from a decisive victory in Union territory justified an offensive attack. (For this reason, the Battle of Antietam was the first battle of the Civil War to be fought on Union soil.) Despite Lee's audacity, his defeat ought to have been nearly guaranteed: not only did the Union army outnumber Lee's forces nearly two to one, but McClellan had an extraordinary stroke of good fortune before the battle. Two of his soldiers found a bundle of cigars that had been dropped on the ground near their encampment; opening the bundle, they discovered that the cigars were wrapped in papers containing Lee's battle plans. This intelligence indicated that Lee had divided his army into three smaller forces spread across northern Virginia, West Virginia, and Maryland, thereby giving McClellan the opportunity to engage each isolated force separately, with overwhelming numerical majority.

However, for reasons that were never made clear, McClellan did not act on this intelligence immediately, instead waiting almost an entire day before giving the order to pursue the Confederates into Maryland. An entire day of bloody fighting ensued, with catastrophic casualties on both sides: around 2000 Union soldiers were killed and another 10,000 were wounded, while Confederate losses numbered around 1,500 dead and 10,000 wounded, not counting the thousands who died of their wounds shortly after the battle. The Battle of Antietam constituted the greatest number of Americans killed or wounded in battle in a single day in all of U.S. military history. The outcome of the battle did not constitute a decisive win for either the Union or the Confederacy. By all reasonable accounts, McClellan ought to have had an easy victory, but his hesitance to take the offensive, combined with the mid-day arrival of Confederate relief troops from Lee's army in

Harper's Ferry, resulted in a stalemate. However, because the Confederate army was the first to retreat, Union propagandists hailed the battle as a victory for the north.

Both Lincoln and his Secretary of War Edwin Stanton expected McClellan to pursue the Confederate army in retreat, and ordered him to do so by telegram. McClellan, however, insisted that his forces were too depleted and disorganized to do so immediately. When he finally attempted a pursuit, it took his forces nine days merely to cross the Potomac River. Frustrated beyond the point where reconciliation with his appointed general was possible, Lincoln removed McClellan from his command on November 5, 1862, and placed the Army of the Potomac under the leadership of General Ambrose Burnside.

The Emancipation Proclamation

On January 1, 1863, Lincoln released to the public a presidential order which he had composed early in 1862: the Emancipation Proclamation, which declared the freedom of every slave living in the Confederate states. The Emancipation Proclamation was not the first measure Lincoln had taken in an attempt to deprive Southern slave owners of their human property. After the first Battle of Bull Run, it became evident to Union military leadership that slaves were crucial to the Confederate war effort; they had watched as slaves performed manual labor for the Confederate army, thereby freeing every available white soldier to pick up a gun and fight. The Confiscation Acts were born as a result. The first Act declared that all Confederate property could legally be confiscated by the Union army—including human property. The second Confiscation Act explicitly stated that the slaves of all Confederate officials, both in the government and in the army, were now legally freed. Furthermore, in the same year, Congress passed an order (at Lincoln's request) which overturned the Fugitive Slave Act of 1850, by making it illegal for Union officers to return runaway slaves to their masters (if their masters were Confederate secessionists.) The Emancipation Proclamation, when it came, was the next natural escalation in the plan to deprive the South of the enormous advantage of unpaid slave labor: it declared that all slaves in Confederate states then in rebellion against the Union were legally free.

The timing of the order was deliberate. Lincoln felt that the order should not come until the army won a decisive Union victory on the battlefield; otherwise it might appear that the federal government was seeking to take revenge on the South for having the superior army. The Battle of Antietam, in November of 1862, was the first significant Union victory after a long run of defeats; the Emancipation Proclamation was released a month and a half later.

Lincoln's attitude towards slavery was complicated. As a private individual, he repudiated slavery as an evil; but as president, he felt that he was legally bound to abide by the laws of the land. Slaves were legally the property of their owners, and the government could not deprive private individuals of their property without just cause, such as punishment for a criminal act, or compensation for the lost property. Furthermore, the President could not legally abolish slavery in the South without the consent of Southern voters. This had been Lincoln's stance on slavery at the time he was elected president; however, the rebellion of the southern states changed the legal situation somewhat. Lincoln took an unprecedented view of the scope of the executive powers allotted to the president during war time; it was his stance that as commander-in-chief of the army, he could take whatever measures he deemed necessary to strengthen the Union's military position.

Thus, the Emancipation Proclamation, like the Confiscation Acts before it, had an express military purpose: without slave labor to prop them up, the Confederacy was considerably weaker. Naturally, there were logistical problems with enacting the Proclamation. The slaves must first escape from their masters (and the reach of any other white southerners) and make it to the Union lines before their freedom was anything more than an idea expressed on paper. Most of the able bodied white men who could have subdued them were away from home, fighting in the Confederate army, but slave overseers were exempt from military service; therefore, flight to Union lines was not without risk.

There were limitations to the Emancipation Proclamation, the most important of which was that the order of release only applied to slaves who lived in the states which had seceded from the Union. Slaves who lived in the so-called "border states" of Maryland, Delaware, Kentucky, and Missouri, where slavery was legal but which were loyal to the Union, were not affected by the Proclamation, just as they had not been affected by the Confiscation Acts. Furthermore, by early 1863, the government of Tennessee had been restored to Union control; slaves who lived there were also not affected by the new ruling, even though Tennessee had seceded. The same restriction applied to West Virginia, and certain parishes in Louisiana. However, the Proclamation made one final, extraordinary provision: it stated that free blacks "of suitable condition" would be permitted to join the Union army. This was a crucial step in revolutionizing the status of free black men. The Dred Scott decision had stated that free blacks could not be citizens, but it became more difficult to argue that black people were not true American citizens after they had fought side by side with white men and taken the same risks on behalf of their country.

A portion of the transcription of the Emancipation Proclamation is reproduced below:

"Now, therefore I, Abraham Lincoln, President of the United States, by virtue of the power in me vested as Commander-in-Chief, of the Army and Navy of the United States in time of actual armed rebellion against the authority and government of the United States, and as a fit and necessary war measure for suppressing said rebellion, do, on this first day of January, in the year of our Lord one thousand eight hundred and sixty-three, and in accordance with my purpose so to do publicly proclaimed for the full period of one hundred days, from the day first above mentioned, order and designate as the States and parts of States wherein the people thereof respectively, are this day in rebellion against the United States[...]

"And by virtue of the power, and for the purpose aforesaid, I do order and declare that all persons held as slaves within said designated States, and parts of States, are, and henceforward shall be free; and that the Executive government of the United States, including the military and naval authorities thereof, will recognize and maintain the freedom of said persons. And I hereby enjoin upon the people so declared to be free to abstain from all violence, unless in necessary self-defence; and I recommend to them that, in all cases when allowed, they labor faithfully for reasonable wages. And I further declare and make known, that such persons of suitable condition, will be received into the armed service of the United States to garrison forts, positions, stations, and other places, and to man vessels of all sorts in said service.

"And upon this act, sincerely believed to be an act of justice, warranted by the Constitution, upon military necessity, I invoke the considerate judgment of mankind, and the gracious favor of Almighty God."

Ulysses S. Grant

Lincoln was unlucky in his generals for most of the war. He did not meet with a commander with whom he could work closely until he appointed Ulysses S. Grant head of all the Union armies following his victory at the Battle of Vicksburg in March of 1864.

Grant was born in Point Pleasant, Ohio, on April 27, 1822, the oldest of six children. His father was a tanner who owned a small farm in Ohio. He was descended from the Pilgrims who settled the Massachusetts Bay Colony in 1630. Grant was admitted to West Point at the age of 17, and graduated in 1843. He changed his name when he became a student: he had been named Hiram

Ulysses by his parents, but Congressman Thomas L. Hamer, whose recommendation enabled him to be admitted to the military academy, mistakenly wrote the name "Ulysses S. Grant" on his letter of recommendation. (The "S" stood for "Simpson", Grant's mother's maiden name.) Grant chose to go by this version of his name for the rest of his life.

Somewhat surprisingly for one of the most famous generals of the Civil War, Grant did not take strongly to the military life. After leaving West Point, he entered the army and was stationed in Missouri at Jefferson Barracks, the largest army stronghold on the American frontier at the time, but he declared his intention to leave the military as soon as his term of enlistment was up and pursue another profession, possibly teaching. However, when the Mexican-American War began in 1846, Grant's unit was transferred to Louisiana, under the command of future U.S. president Zachary

Taylor (this would have placed him nearby future Confederate president Jefferson Davis, who also fought under Taylor's command.) Grant carried out several high risk assignments during the war, including riding on horseback through the line of fire to deliver a field dispatch. In recognition of his exceptional bravery, Grant won a brevet field promotion to the rank of captain. His conduct during the war was rendered all the more remarkable by the fact that he considered the conflict a morally unjustifiable aggression by the United States against a weaker nation for the purpose of attaining land and expanding slavery.

After the war, Grant married the sister of one of his West Point classmates, a woman named Julia Dent. Initially, Grant remained a soldier, and was transferred with his wife and growing family to various military bases around the country, until 1854, when he was asked to resign his commission after appearing at dinner at the officer's dining hall in an obvious state of drunkenness. The seven intervening years between his resignation from the army and the outbreak of the Civil War were difficult ones for Grant. Initially, he and his family retreated to the Missouri plantation where Julia Grant had grown up, but Grant went to work in his father's leather goods shop after he found himself unable to make a living as a farmer.

While opposed to the secession of the southern states, Grant was not especially political prior to the outbreak of the war. However, he was deeply shocked when Confederate soldiers fired on Ft. Sumter, and when Lincoln's call for 75,000 army volunteers went out to the states, Grant was asked to assist in the formation and training of a volunteer regiment, because of his prior military experience. Between April and June of 1861, Grant tried unsuccessfully to gain an officer's commission, but he found that his reputation for drunkenness preceded him. That summer, however, he was made a colonel and placed in command of a regiment; two months later he was promoted to brigadier general. Grant spent the first two years of the war fighting in the western theater, achieving significant victories throughout Tennessee, including a successful attack against Ft. Donelson, a Confederate stronghold that overlooked the Cumberland river. In a famous incident that was reported in newspapers throughout the North, Ft. Donelson's Confederate commander send Grant a message asking what terms he would accept for their surrender. Grant replied that nothing but an immediate and unconditional surrender would do, and thereafter it was said that his initials, U.S., stood for "Unconditional Surrender".

The Battle of Shiloh

The Union Army of Tennessee met with a series of victories early in the war that resulted in its becoming the first Confederate state that was returned to Union control; this was largely due to Grant's able military leadership. After the Union gained control of the strategically crucial Cumberland river following the attack on Ft. Donelson, Confederate forces under Pierre Beauregard regrouped in the town of Corinth, in Mississippi, an important center for the railroad lines that communicated between the deep South and the west. Grant's army outnumbered the Confederate army more than two to one, but at dawn on April 6, 1862, General Albert Sydney Johnston led a surprise attack on Grant's forces. The Confederate objective was to drive the Union army out of the region and into the swamps. However, on the second day of the battle, April 7, the Army of the Ohio, under the command of General Don Carlos Buell, arrived to reinforce Grant's men, and together the Union armies were able to retake all the ground they had lost to the Confederates the day before.

Casualties at the Battle of Shiloh were heavy, amounting to 14,000 killed or wounded on the

Union side alone. On the Confederate side, General Johnston suffered a bullet wound to the leg which struck the femoral artery; he bled out and died while commanding his troops on the field. A Union victory was declared, but Grant's reputation suffered when word traveled east that he had allowed himself to be taken by surprise by the Union attack. Some newspapers suggested that he had been unprepared for the battle because he had been drinking. Lincoln, however, ignored demands that Grant be removed from his command, famously remarking, "I can't spare this man; he fights." Grant's command style was to vigorously pursue the enemy, a marked contrast to George McClellan's refusal to engage Confederate forces. This probably inclined Lincoln to be lenient towards any perceived personal shortcomings Grant may have possessed.

Siege of Vicksburg

While Union territory was concentrated largely in the northeast, Confederate territory extended broadly to the west. The Mississippi River, the south's most strategically important waterway, formed the borders that divided Louisiana from Mississippi, Arkansas from Tennessee, Missouri from Illinois, and Kentucky from Indiana and Ohio. In 1862, the fortified city of Vicksburg, which lay near the Mississippi Delta, was the Confederacy's last stronghold on the river; Jefferson Davis referred to the town as "the nail head that holds the South's two halves together". Retaining control of this portion of the Mississippi was immensely important to the Confederate army. If it was lost to the Union, they would no longer be able to received supplies or reinforcements from Texas and the surroundings areas.

After the Battle of Shiloh, Grant temporarily lost his command, but it was restored in time for the beginning of the Union assault on Vicksburg, which lasted for several months, from December of 1862 to January of 1863, and then again from

March to July of 1863. At first, Union warships bombarded the city, but to no avail. A ground assault by Union forces also met with defeat. Vicksburg was situated on a bluff, which gave the Confederate forces inside the city a natural defense against incursion. Eventually, Grant maneuvered the Army of the Tennessee around Vicksburg, south to Louisiana, where they rendezvoused with a fleet of Union warships under the command of Rear Admiral David Dixon Porter; Porter's fleet had run the Vicksburg gun battery, an incredibly daring move that relied on deft maneuvering to evade heavy fire. Grant's army boarded the ships, which ferried them from the west bank to the east. There, they began an inland campaign, capturing the Mississippi capital of Jackson. After a number of skirmishes in the areas surrounding Vicksburg, Grant ordered a siege of the city, cutting it off from all outside supplies. Vicksburg was garrisoned by 9,000 Confederate soldiers; the combined Union forces amounted to over 70,000. They advanced on the city slowly, digging trenches as shields against gunfire. Finally, on July 4, 1863, Grant permitted Confederate General John C. Pemberton to surrender on terms that allowed 30,000 of his men to go free on parole. The Union army now stood in complete control of the Mississippi River, and the Confederacy was split in half, east and west. Shortly after the end of the siege, Grant received a letter from Abraham Lincoln, who, in a year's time, would install him as the commander of the entire Union army:

"I do not remember that you and I ever met personally. I write this now as a grateful acknowledgment for the almost inestimable service you have done the country. I wish to say a word further. When you first reached the vicinity of Vicksburg, I thought you should do, what you finally did—march the troops across the neck, run the batteries with the transports, and thus go below; and I never had any faith, except a general hope that you knew better than I, that the Yazoo Pass expedition, and the like, could succeed. When you got below, and took Port Gibson, Grand Gulf, and vicinity, I thought you should go down the river and join Gen. Banks; and when you turned Northward East of the Big Black, I feared it was a mistake. I now wish to make the personal acknowledgment that you were right, and I was wrong."

Confederate casualties at Vicksburg were comparatively light, considering the duration of the campaign, numbering under two thousand. However, the loss of Vicksburg was an inestimable strategic blow in the west. And it was not the only such blow to befall the Confederacy that week; the day before Pemberton's surrender, Robert E. Lee's northern campaign had come to a bloody end on a certain Pennsylvania battlefield which would afterwards become the Civil War's most famous symbol.

Gettysburg

The Army of the Potomac changed commanders five times during the course of the Civil War. Irvin McDowell was replaced by George McClellan, who was replaced by Ambrose Burnisde; Joseph Hooker was the commander for six months in 1863, followed by General George G. Meade, who led the army for exactly two years, from June 28, 1863 to June 28 1865. Just three days after Meade assumed command, he led Union forces in battle against the Confederate Army of Northern Virginia in what would eventually become known as the bloodiest, most important, and later the famous battle of the war—Gettysburg.

For two months in the late summer of 1862 Lee's forces had enjoyed a series of battlefield victories which drove the Union army under McClellan out of peninsular Virginia. Lee had attempted to invade the North during the so called Maryland Campaign, only to be forced into a retreat at the Battle of Antietam, but his recent victories against Ambrose Burnside at Fredericksburg and against Joseph Hooker at Chancellorsville emboldened him to make a second attempt. Lee his sights on organizing a second northern invasion, this time pressing as far into Union territory as Pennsylvania. Lee's major objective was to place the Baltimore & Ohio railroad line, which connected the major Union port city of Baltimore to the federal capital of Washington, in Confederate hands. His secondary goal was to draw Union forces away from Vicksburg, where Grant's Union forces were laying siege to the city. Control of Vicksburg meant control of the Mississippi River; control of both the railroad and the river would virtually guarantee the outcome of the war for whichever side possessed them.

After Hooker's defeat at Chancellorsville, Lincoln placed Meade in control of the Army of the Potomac with explicit instructions to follow Lee into Pennsylvania and halt his advance. When

Lee got wind of Meade's pursuit, he began making arrangement for all Confederate forces in the area to regroup at the town of Gettysburg, but when the advanced guard arrived, it discovered that Meade's men had beaten them there. July 1—the first day of the three day battle—was fought between the first Confederate division and the two Union advance brigades, but miscommunication between Lee and one of his subordinates saved the Union forces from a rout. They retreated to a nearby area known as Cemetery Ridge, where they were joined by the rest of the Union army the next day. On July 2, full scale conflict ensued, resulting in nearly 9000 casualties on both the Union and Confederate sides.

On July 3, Lee ordered an offensive assault against the center of the Union line, over the protests of his second in command. Led by General George Pickett, a division of some 15,000 soldiers marched into the line of fire while the Union soldiers took aim from the shelter of stone battlements. Between half and three quarters of Pickett's men were killed; the advance would come to be known as "Pickett's Charge", and blame for the overwhelming losses sustained by the division would follow Pickett for the rest of his life. After the third day of fighting came to a close, Lee was forced to acknowledge that his second attempted northern invasion had no chance of success. The next day, July 4, Lee's forces retreated south to Virginia. In what was fast becoming a recurring theme with Lincoln's chosen generals, Meade elected not to pursue the remnants of Lee's army. By the end of the fighting, Union casualties amounted to some 23,000 killed or wounded, with approximately 28,000 casualties on the Confederate side. Not only was Gettysburg the bloodiest battle of the Civil War, but it together with the fall of Vicksburg on July 3, its outcome had turned the tide of the conflict decisively in the Union's favor. Nonetheless, fighting would continue for another two years.

Five months later, to commemorate the catastrophic loss of American lives on the Gettysburg battlefield, a group of lawyers and businessmen raised money to dedicate the battlefield as a national cemetery. In order to lend gravity to the occasion, they invited a famous orator to give a long address; Abraham Lincoln was also invited to make a few remarks. Lincoln was not popular for the first three years of his first term in office. The war had gone badly for the Union for a long time, and the public blamed the president for not ending the conflict more swiftly. After Gettysburg, however, public opinion changed, and Lincoln was praised for the mounting Union victories. The two minute long speech he delivered at Gettysburg, addressed mainly to the families of the soldiers who had died there, is now the most enduring relic of the battle. The text of Lincoln's Gettysburg Address is reproduced below:

"Four score and seven years ago our fathers brought forth on this continent a new nation, conceived in liberty, and dedicated to the proposition that all men are created equal.

"Now we are engaged in a great civil war, testing whether that nation, or any nation so conceived and so dedicated, can long endure. We are met on a great battlefield of that war. We have come to dedicate a portion of that field, as a final resting place for those who here gave their lives that that nation might live. It is altogether fitting and proper that we should do this.

"But, in a larger sense, we can not dedicate, we can not consecrate, we can not hallow this ground. The brave men, living and dead, who struggled here, have consecrated it, far above our poor power to add or detract. The world will little note, nor long remember what we say here, but it can never forget what they did here. It is for us the living, rather, to be dedicated here to the unfinished work which they who fought here have thus far so nobly advanced. It is rather for us to be here dedicated to the great task remaining before us—that from these honored dead we take increased devotion to that cause for which they gave the last full measure of devotion—that we here highly resolve that these dead shall not have died in vain—that this nation, under God, shall have a new birth of freedom—and that government of the people, by the people, for the people, shall not perish from the earth."

Chapter Four: The Road to Peace

In March of 1864, Lincoln appointed Ulysses S. Grant as the commander of all the Union armies under the rank of Lieutenant General, a rank that was created for George Washington when he held command of the U.S. army from the end of his second term as president, until his death. Replacing Grant in the western theater of the war was General William T. Sherman. In May of that year, Grant and Sherman coordinated a massive military campaign designed to rout the Confederate armies once and for all. Throughout May and early June, Grant's army of 120,000 men advanced towards the Confederate capital of Richmond to engage Lee's Army of Northern Virginia, which had dwindled to only half the size of Grant's forces. Meanwhile, Sherman began a campaign pushing east with 100,000 men from Tennessee to Atlanta, Georgia, where he would engage Confederate forces led by Joseph E. Johnston.

Sherman's Atlanta Campaign and March to the Sea

In May of 1865, the western Union army was concentrated at Chattanooga, Tennessee, where William T. Sherman began to map out a planned assault on Atlanta, Georgia—the most important rail and manufacturing center in Confederate territory. Joseph E. Johnston's forces were encamped in Dalton, Georgia, not far from Atlanta, but Johnston refused to make any offensive moves again Sherman—rather, he waited while slowly amassing reinforcements in an attempt to balance out the numerical odds. (Sherman's army was larger, but a number of his men were on leave or were wounded, decreasing the actual numbers he had to fight with.)

To the north, Grant's forces were fighting Lee's at every opportunity, as Grant used his 2 to 1 numerical superiority to absorb casualties with greater ease than Lee could afford. Sherman, however, chose not to make a direct assault against Johnston's forces with his full strength; instead, two divisions engaged Johnston in a diversionary battle, while a third division crept around the Confederate flank to attack the railroad line that was supplying Johnston with reinforcements. Between May and June, Sherman's forces attacked so many times that Johnston's army was forced to retreat and regroup in Atlanta.

Around this point, Confederate President Jefferson Davis replaced Johnston with General John Hood, who was far more aggressive and less likely to cede ground to the Union army without a fight. Hood directed two offensive attacks against Sherman's men, the second of which, at Peachtree Creek just outside Atlanta, was nearly successful. The city of Atlanta was surrounded by formidable fortifications; rather than assault them directly, Sherman concentrated his efforts on a push westward, where the sole remaining railroad line coming into Atlanta lay. Hood's men defended the railroad through all of July and August, and eventually Sherman began to bombard the city with artillery. On August 25, Sherman's men were successful in cutting the railroad line, and Hood's men were forced to evacuate Atlanta within a week, on September 1. Sherman took control of the city on September 2.

After fleeing Atlanta, Hood split his army into two commands, both marching west, to Alabama and Tennessee respectively. Sherman sent 60,000 of his troops, under the command of Major General George Thomas, to engage the Confederate Army of Tennessee at Nashville. The other 62,000 Sherman led personally in an advance towards Savannah, in what has come to be known as Sherman's March to the Sea.

Sherman's strategy was to deliver a crushing blow to the morale of white Southern civilians by destroying their farms and factories and generally wreaking as much destruction as humanly possible. They stole as much food as they could carry and burned everything they could not use, killing livestock and burning crops, so as to prevent any assistance being given to Confederate troops. Sherman believed that these "total war" tactics would bring an end to the conflict much faster than any mere military maneuver against armed soldiers. The destructive power of Sherman's army was so great that the remaining Confederate soldiers in the area stopped trying to fight them, and instead fled ahead to destroy bridges and roads, in an attempt to slow the Union army's progress. Sherman reached Savannah on December 21, 1864, and discovered that the ten thousand Confederate soldiers they had expected to defend the city had fled.

William T. Sherman wrote the following passage in his memoirs regarding the harshness of the "total war" policy:

"You cannot qualify war in harsher terms than I will. War is cruelty, and you cannot refine it; and those who brought war into our country deserve all the curses and maledictions a people can pour out. I know I had no hand in making this war, and I know I will make more sacrifices to-day than any of you to secure peace."

The Thirteenth Amendment

After the fall of Savannah in December of 1864, it became clear to everyone that the war was nearing a close. Confederate vice president Alexander Stephens sent word to Washington that winter that he was interested in conducting peace talks. Lincoln did meet with Stephens in early February of 1865, but his immediate priority was persuading Congress to pass the Thirteenth Amendment.

In 1863, Lincoln had published the Emancipation Proclamation, an executive order issued under Lincoln's expanded war powers, which declared that slaves in the rebellious Confederate states were free under the law. However, slavery remained legal in the four border states which had remained loyal to the Union, and in places like Tennessee and West Virginia, where a Union government had been re-established. Lincoln had justified freeing the slaves owned by Confederates on the grounds that doing so would weaken the economy of the south and the Confederate army itself, which used slaves for military purposes. As the end of the war approached, however, Lincoln was determined to abolish slavery once and for all in the United States. In order to accomplish this, he had to keep Alexander Stephens' offer of peace talks a secret. A majority of Congress was adamantly opposed to abolishing slavery in the border states if the war could be brought to an end without doing so. Lincoln, however, believed that if the issue of slavery was not resolved once and for all during his presidency, it would only be a matter of time before another war broke out. Adding to his motivation was his personal feeling that slavery was a moral evil, and that if by any legal means he could end it, he was duty bound to do so.

Lincoln argued that if slavery were ended throughout the entire country, the Confederacy would lose its will keep fighting. He was opposed, not only by the border states, but by those who saw abolition as the first step on a road that would lead to full citizenship and voting rights for blacks. When the amendment came to a vote, it won by a very narrow margin; Lincoln's Secretary of State, William H. Seward, had awarded a number of bribes and patronage positions to secure the necessary votes. The amendment passed both houses of Congress on January 31, 1865.

The full text of the amendment reads as follows:

"**Section 1.** Neither slavery nor involuntary servitude, except as a punishment for crime whereof the party shall have been duly convicted, shall exist within the United States, or any place subject to their jurisdiction.

Section 2. Congress shall have power to enforce this article by appropriate legislation."

A month later, on February 1, 1864, Lincoln signed the amendment. This was not legally required, since by constitutional law the president plays no role in the passing of constitutional amendments; but in signing it, Lincoln conveyed the message that the amendment had the full support of the executive office.

The Overland Campaign

At the same time that Sherman was embarked on his Atlanta Campaign, Grant was pursuing the Army of Northern Virginia under the command of Robert E. Lee from Pennsylvania into Virginia. Like Sherman, Grant had an army that outnumbered the enemy. Unlike Sherman, Grant was confident that the size of his army alone would ensure victory, provided he sustain the assault for as long as necessary to bring Lee to his knees. Grant was prepared to sustain heavy casualties to make this happen.

From May 5 to June 24 of 1864, Confederate and Union forces in Virginia fought in fourteen distinct battles and skirmishes. Union victory was not always certain. Grant had pushed Lee's men into a corner where they could not be resupplied or relieved by the arrival of new soldiers; because of this, they fought desperately.

The first major battle of the Overland Campaign was known as the Battle of the Wilderness, because it took place in a dense forest. The Confederate troops hid themselves in the tangled trees and underbrush, waiting for the Union army to arrive, so that they could fire from under the cover of the foliage. After two days of fighting, Lee's men retreated. Unlike the Union commanders before him, Grant pursued, assuming that the Confederates were headed for Richmond. However, Lee had anticipated that Grant would follow, and had re-grouped his forces at the Spotsylvania Courthouse, where the Union army found them lying in wait behind a fortification of hastily dug trenches. The fighting at Spotsylvania continued for two weeks, until Grant decided to leave Lee's men where they were and proceed to Richmond. They fought for another two weeks at Cold Harbor, where the Confederates inflicted over 6000 casualties on the Union forces. Grant's final target was the city of Petersburg, a rail center that made it possible for supplies to enter the city of Richmond;

maintaining Confederate control of Petersburg was essential if they were to continue defending the Confederate capital.

The Siege of Petersburg

The siege of Petersburg lasted for nearly ten months. The city was defended by 20,000 Confederate soldiers, while outside the city, around 100,000 Union soldiers were busy digging a system of trenches that fortified them against defensive assaults. Union forces did not succeed in breaking through the Confederate defenses until April of 1865. Lee immediately retreated, and the Confederate government in Richmond moved to Danville, Virginia, near the border with North Carolina. Lee's hope was to march southwest to North Carolina, and combine his army with that of Joseph E. Johnston, which was defending Atlanta against William T. Sherman's army. Grant, however, pursued Lee so closely that Lee's army never made it to North Carolina.

A number of small battles and skirmishes in the area around the Appomattox river cut Lee's numbers down further and further. Eventually, Grant wrote Lee a short note, asking him to consider the possibility of surrender, the text of which has been reproduced below:

"The results of the last week must convince you of the hopelessness of further resistance on the part of the Army of Northern Virginia in this struggle. I feel that it is so, and regard it as my duty to shift from myself the responsibility of any further effusion of blood by asking of you the surrender of that portion of the Confederate States army known as the Army of Northern Virginia."

Lee replied to this note by requesting that Grant specify what terms of surrender he would find acceptable. After exchanging several more messages over the next day and evening, Lee sent a message to Grant requesting a face to face meeting. According to observers, Grant was suffering from a bad migraine when he received this note, which vanished as soon as he read it. He replied to Lee, asking him to name a location for the interview.

Surrender At Appomattox

On April 9, 1865, Lee surrendered his army to Grant at Appomattox, Virginia. Lee and Grant met for a discussion of the terms of surrender at the home of a local man named Wilmer McLean, where Grant mentioned to Lee that they had met once before, during the Mexican-American War. Lee replied that he recalled the meeting, and had often tried to remember what Grant looked like since then. Lee then asked for Grant to write out the specific terms on which he would accept a surrender. The following quote contains the terms that Grant wrote out in Lee's presence:

"In accordance with the substance of my letter to you of the 8th inst., I propose to receive the surrender of the Army of N. Va. on the following terms, to wit: Rolls of all the officers and men to be made in duplicate. One copy to be given to an officer designated by me, the other to be retained by such officer or officers as you may designate. The officers to give their individual paroles not to take up arms against the Government of the United States until properly exchanged, and each company or regimental commander sign a like parole for the men of their commands. The arms, artillery and public property to be parked and stacked, and turned over to the officer appointed by me to receive them. This will not embrace the side-arms of the officers, nor their private horses or baggage. This done, each officer and man will be allowed to return to their homes, not to be disturbed by United States authority so long as they observe their paroles and the laws in force where they may reside."

Relieved that his men would not be taken prisoner or charged with treason, Lee accepted Grant's terms, and wrote out a formal letter indicating his acceptance. When Lee rode away, the Union soldiers began to cheer, but Grant ordered them to stop; his feeling was that now that the Confederate army had surrendered, they were once again all citizens of the same country, and it was unseemly to rejoice in a countryman's downfall. A formal ceremony of surrender followed, in which the Confederate soldiers stacked their weapons, except for the officers' personal sidearms, in a pile under the observation of the Union officers.

When news of Lee's surrender traveled south, the remaining Confederate forces lost heart for further fighting. The only remaining Confederate army of any substantial size was Joseph E. Johnston's army, which had retreated into North Carolina to evade William T. Sherman's march to the sea. Weeks after Lee's surrender, on April 18, Johnston surrendered to Sherman at Durham, North Carolina.

Assassination of Abraham Lincoln

Though fighting continued after Lee's surrender on April 9, 1865, the Civil War had essentially come to an end. On April 10, word of the surrender reached Washington, and the people took to the streets in celebration. On April 14, the Union flag was raised in a ceremony over Ft. Sumter, signifying a symbolic end to the war. However, Abraham Lincoln did not live to see the surrender of the last remaining Confederate armies. He was shot by John Wilkes Booth two days before the end of the fighting in the upper south, on April 14, and he died early the next morning, on April 15.

On the evening he was shot, Lincoln and his wife, Mary Todd Lincoln, were attending a performance of a play called "Our American

Cousin" at Ford's Theater in Washington.
Lincoln had requested that his bodyguards not
accompany him that evening, which was not
uncommon. He was well aware of the many
death threats he had received over the course of
his presidency, but did not take them very
seriously; in his opinion, there was no way to
prevent his being killed, so long as the assassin
was himself willing to die in the attempt.

John Wilkes Booth was an out of work actor
from the south with some professional ties to
Ford's Theater. Booth considered Lincoln
responsible for the war and the ruin of the south.
He had not enlisted in the Confederate army
himself, by the request of his mother, but once
the war ended he felt shamed by the fact that he
had never served in uniform. Booth had been
fixated on Lincoln for some time, and had
actually formed a plot to kidnap him a few
months before. The plot had fallen apart, but
elements of it played a role in the assassination—

for instance, he made use of the same escape route he had plotted out for spiriting Lincoln away to a cabin in Maryland.

Shortly before the assassination, Booth had been present at a speech Lincoln made after returning from meeting Grant in Richmond. In this speech, Lincoln had made reference to the possibility of voting enfranchisement for blacks, and as Booth was adamantly against freedom for slaves and rights for free blacks, this probably motivated the assassination to a certain degree. His intent was to murder not only Lincoln, but also Secretary of State William H. Seward and Vice President Andrew Johnson, but they had not accompanied Lincoln to the theater. Seward had actually changed his plans to attend because he felt it would be dangerous for him to appear in public, and he had tried to persuade Lincoln to cancel as well.

Booth did not encounter many obstacles on the path to assassination. He crept quietly into Lincoln's theater box, and not until he shot the president in the back of the head did anyone notice his presence. A Major Rathbone, who was attending the play with his fiancée as the Lincolns' guest, grappled with Booth, who escaped after slashing him in the arm with a dagger. Booth jumped down to the stage, shouting to the confused audience, who did not yet realize what had happened; he fractured his leg on landing. Booth then ran from the theater and mounted a horse, which had been made ready for him, and fled to Maryland. A frenzied search for Booth commenced immediately, as Secretary of War Edwin Stanton issued a $100,000 reward for his capture. After eleven days of fleeing through the countryside from one hiding spot to the next, Booth was eventually tracked down to a tobacco barn in Port Royal, Virginia, by a regiment of Union soldiers on April 26, 1865. When Booth refused to surrender, the barn was set on fire; Booth charged from the barn shooting his pistol, and was shot in the neck. The shot paralyzed him, and he died a few hours later.

Lincoln's body was prepared for a three week funeral procession crossing the country from Washington to Springfield, Illinois, his home town. The remains of his son William, who had died a few years earlier at the White House, were disinterred and placed in the coffin with the body of his father. The processional route took Lincoln's coffin from Washington, to Baltimore, then to Pennsylvania and New York, then to Ohio, Indiana, and then Illinois. Thousands of people across the country amassed to their pay respects to the procession.

Conclusion: After the War
Andrew Johnson

Lincoln died just over a month into his second term in office. His vice president, Andrew Johnson, was new to his position, having replaced Hannibal Hamlin, who had been vice president during Lincoln's first term. Johnson was a "War Democrat"—as a senator from Tennessee, he had been the only member of Congress from a seceding state to remain loyal to the Union. After Tennessee seceded, Johnson had resigned his seat in Congress and returned home, where he Lincoln appointed him governor after a Union military government had been established there.

Like Lincoln, Johnson had no formal education, and had worked in a trade prior to entering politics. Unlike Lincoln, he had owned slaves and supported the rights of states to make slavery legal within their own borders. Lincoln's political partnership with Johnson was intended to send the message that there was still a place in the Union for those who disagreed with the president's policies.

Reconstruction

After Lincoln's death, Johnson was sworn in as the seventeenth president of the United States. His immediate focus was necessarily Reconstruction—in other words, re-integrating the former Confederate states into the Union. Lincoln had been making plans along these lines at the time of this death; he favored the so-called "ten percent plan", wherein elections would be restored in the southern states as soon as ten percent of a state's population took an oath of loyalty to the Union.

The majority of Congress, however, believed that the South deserved some form of punishment for their rebellion. Radical Republicans wanted the country's newly freed black citizens to be given full voting rights as soon as possible; centrist

Republicans opposed southern Democrats holding office; and Democrats in the north believed that the former Confederate states should be returned to the Union with all their rights intact. Johnson's agenda was somewhat simpler; he wanted to be re-elected president in his own right. Voting rights for new black citizens was a matter he was content to leave in the hands of the states. Prior to Congress re-convening in December of 1865, Johnson authorized elections in the south and granted amnesty to all Confederates who owned property valued at less than $20,000.

The Black Codes

The status of blacks, not only in the former Confederate states, but in the nation as a whole, was left undetermined for many years after the war. Blacks were no longer slaves, but they also weren't citizens or legally the equal of whites. All the anxieties which had existed before the war regarding "troublesome" free black populations were heightened when slavery was abolished.

The belief that free blacks would create crime and danger in any city where they settled made it nearly impossible for former slaves to begin new lives in the south, where they had lived all their lives. Most did not have the means to move north or west, where conditions were somewhat better.

In the south, most slaves were still economically dependent on their former masters. Unable to obtain paying jobs in the cities, blacks were often forced to sign labor contracts that restricted their movements and pledged their working availability to an infrastructure that had yet to evolve past the point of being dependent on unpaid labor. Beginning with South Carolina and Mississippi, the southern states created "black codes"—laws that pertained only to blacks, and which served to control them nearly as much as if they had still been slaves. In South Carolina specifically, blacks were prohibited by law from taking any job other than that of a farmhand or a domestic servant, unless they paid a high yearly tax.

Other laws restricted the rights of blacks to participate in civic institutions; for instance, black men were only permitted to serve on juries if both the defendant and plaintiff in the case were also black. Vagrancy laws were created to penalize any black person who could not prove that they had a paying job, which made it nearly impossible for blacks to extricate themselves from exploitative labor contracts. As late as the early twentieth century, many blacks who had been arrested for vagrancy or on even flimsier pretexts were forced to work as de facto slaves for white land owners; this was permitted on the legal argument that slavery had been outlawed except as a punishment for crime. Not until after World War II, and to a much greater extent the Civil Rights era of the 1960's, did black Americans see an easing of the restrictions which prevented them from living on equal terms with whites.

Afterword

It is difficult to acknowledge the extent of institutional racism in the United States today unless one has a decent grasp of American history, including an awareness of the role that slavery played in shaping the country. This is precisely why the myths about the Civil War—such as the theory that the Confederacy fought for "states' rights" rather than slavery, or the notion that the Union fought primarily to free the slaves—are so entrenched in popular thinking. It is difficult to find anyone alive today who does not understand that slavery was an unthinkable abuse of human rights. And for that very reason, we avoid thinking about it. The states' rights myth seeks to absolve our ancestors of some degree of culpability in having participated in slavery. The myth that the Union fought to free the slaves allows us to believe that at least half the country understood that slavery was wrong. The reality is that the majority of white Americans did not begin to grasp the evils of slavery until after it had already been abolished. This seems like an important lesson that we should have been taught in our high school history classes—so why didn't we learn it there?

A common reaction that we find whenever the topic of slavery is raised in discussions about society today goes something like this: "My ancestors didn't own slaves. We were too poor, or we didn't live in this country yet. Why should I feel responsible?" This line of logic misses the point. One does not need to feel overwhelmed by personal guilt over the fact that one's great-grandfather was a slave owner in order to acknowledge that the United States as we know it today was shaped by slaves—built on their labor, their exploited talents, and their suffering. It is a fact that lies beyond any dispute. We cannot change the past, but we can do something far more profitable: we can examine our present, and use the lessons that history teaches us to ask questions about "domestic institutions" that exist today.

One of the most psychologically fascinating aspects of the Civil War, in the opinion of the author, is the fact that, as the south grew more and more economically dependent on slavery, the rhetoric around slavery changed. When America was founded, slave owners like George Washington wrote frankly about their distaste for it. For Washington, slavery was a grim necessity; he could not liberate his slaves without ruining himself financially, but the whole business of owning several hundred human beings depressed him. This attitude stands in marked contrast to the attitudes of people like Alexander Stephens, eighty years later, who declared that slavery was a positive good, that it needed to exist, that it was God's will and that all Christians should support it. The fact that slavery began to be seen as a good thing at exactly the same time that the southern economy began to become more dependent on it suggests something rather frightening about human nature. Do we always come to believe that things are good because they are useful, or helpful, or more convenient than the alternative? And if that is the case, then what institutions in our society today do we justify as morally right, only because it would inconvenient to get rid of them?

It is worth noting that the language of the Thirteenth Amendment outlaws slavery, defined as involuntary servitude, in every case except as punishment for crime. In the United States today, prisoners can be forced to work as cheap or unpaid labor on threat of solitary confinement. Many big businesses, such as Wal Mart, are able to offer cheap goods to customers because they buy their stock from for-profit prisons. According to U.S. Census statistics, black men and women are five times more likely to go to prison as whites. Does this constitute slave labor? Many people would say no; others would say that forced labor is a reasonable punishment for people who break the law. There may not be an easy answer, but this, again, is the role of history—what a nation has done in the past, it is likely to do again.

Today, the American south continues to be plagued with problems that are a direct result of its involvement in the Civil War. Poverty rates for both blacks and whites are higher than elsewhere in the United States. In 2015, massive protests against police brutality that targets black youths broke out in Ferguson, Missouri, and Baltimore, Maryland. Maryland and Missouri, you will remember from earlier in this book, are both former "border states"—the Union states where slavery remained legal until the passing of the Thirteenth Amendment. Is it a coincidence that the areas of the country where slavery survived unchallenged for longer than anywhere are currently the areas of the country where racism and racial unrest are at their strongest? Again, there may not be a simple answer. But a knowledge of America's troubled history will equip you to address these questions with greater confidence.

It is also worth remembering that Abraham Lincoln, who is remembered today as the greatest of all American presidents, didn't get everything right according to modern standards of anti-racist thinking. Had the south not seceded from the Union, he probably would have passed his whole presidency without attempting to abolish slavery throughout the entire country. And even though he seized the opportunity provided by the Civil War to issue the Emancipation Proclamation and advocate for the passage of the Thirteenth Amendment, he never changed his opinion on the inherent racial inferiority of blacks as compared to whites. Lincoln was not confident that free blacks could ever live in the United States without great suffering; he tried to convince black leaders such as Frederick Douglass that former slaves would be happier if they left the country and emigrated to places such as Liberia, in Africa. But we can draw this useful lesson from Lincoln's example: that even if future generations look back on our opinions and ideas and consider them backwards, we can still do important things in the cause of justice, as long as we try, and remember to be compassionate. After all, it wasn't a stirring political speech that made Lincoln oppose slavery; he realized that slavery was wrong when he was a very young man, working on a river boat that took him south to New Orleans, where he saw a slave auction for the first time. All he had to do was see how much suffering slaves endured; compassion taught him what he had to do next.

The words of Lincoln's second inaugural address, delivered only a few weeks before he was assassinated, summarize the most important lessons we can derive from a study of the Civil War.

"If we shall suppose that American slavery is one of those offenses which, in the providence of God, must needs come, but which, having continued through His appointed time, He now wills to remove, and that He gives to both North and South this terrible war as the woe due to those by whom the offense came, shall we discern therein any departure from those divine attributes which the believers in a living God always ascribe to Him? Fondly do we hope, fervently do we pray, that this mighty scourge of war may speedily pass away. Yet, if God wills that it continue until all the wealth piled by the bondsman's two hundred and fifty years of unrequited toil shall be sunk, and until every drop of blood drawn with the lash shall be paid by another drawn with the sword, as was said three thousand years ago, so still it must be said "the judgments of the Lord are true and righteous altogether."

"With malice toward none, with charity for all, with firmness in the right as God gives us to see the right, let us strive on to finish the work we are in, to bind up the nation's wounds, to care for him who shall have borne the battle and for his widow and his orphan, to do all which may achieve and cherish a just and lasting peace among ourselves and with all nations."

Works Referenced

The Cornerstone Speech

http://teachingamericanhistory.org/library/document/cornerstone-speech/

Narrative of the Life of Frederick Douglass, An American Slave

http://www.gutenberg.org/ebooks/23

The Confessions of Nat Turner

http://www.gutenberg.org/files/15333/15333-h/15333-h.htm

The Relationship Between Abraham Lincoln and Owen Lovejoy

http://www.lovejoysociety.org/Lincoln/Lincoln_Lovejoy_relationship.htm

A Declaration of the Immediate Causes Which May Induce and Justify the Secession of South Carolina from the Federal Union

http://www.teachingushistory.org/lessons/DecofImCauses.htm

Dates of Secession of the Southern States

http://www.libs.uga.edu/hargrett/selections/co
nfed/dates.html

Article IV of the Constitution of the United
States

https://www.law.cornell.edu/constitution/articl
eiv

Governor Letcher's Proclamation.; His Reply to
Secretary Cameron—State of Affairs at Norfolk

http://www.nytimes.com/1861/04/22/news/gov
-letcher-s-proclamation-his-reply-secretary-
cameron-state-affairs-norfolk.html

Lincoln's Proclamation of Blockade of Southern
Ports

http://www.presidency.ucsb.edu/ws/?pid=7010
1

Lincoln's Proclamation Calling for 500,000
Volunteers

http://www.presidency.ucsb.edu/ws/?pid=6999
6

The South's Shocking History: Thousands of
Blacks Forced Into Slavery Until WW2

http://www.alternet.org/civil-liberties/souths-
shocking-hidden-history-thousands-blacks-
forced-slavery-until-ww2#.Vq-7QQWY37w.